Adolph Lurie has had more than fifty years' experience in accounting, auditing, and financial reporting as a financial executive and professional CPA.

ADOLPH LURIE

HOW TO READ ANNUAL REPORTS

Intelligently

A STOCKHOLDER'S GUIDE

A SPECTRUM BOOK

Prentice-Hall, Inc., Englewood Cliffs, New Jersey

Library of Congress Cataloging in Publication Data

Lurie, Adolph G.
  How to read annual reports—intelligently.

  "A Spectrum Book."
  Includes index.
  1. Corporation reports.   I. Title.
HG4028.B2L87   1984   338.7'4   84-11719
ISBN 0-13-430562-0
ISBN 0-13-430554-X (pbk.)

This book is available at a special discount when ordered in
bulk quantities. Contact Prentice-Hall, Inc., General
Publishing Division, Special Sales, Englewood Cliffs, N.J. 07632.

1 2 3 4 5 6 7 8 9 10

ISBN 0-13-430562-0

ISBN 0-13-430554-X (PBK.)

Editorial/production supervision: Kimberly Mazur
Cover design: Hal Siegel
Manufacturing buyer: Joyce Levatino

FMC Corporation's 1981 annual report is reprinted courtesy FMC Corporation.
Poem on page ii reprinted from "From Pepper . . . and Salt",
the *Wall Street Journal*, May 26, 1983. © 1983.
Excerpts from annual reports for the Manville Corporation
are reprinted courtesy Manville Corporation.

Prentice-Hall International, Inc., London
Prentice-Hall of Australia Pty. Limited, Sydney
Prentice-Hall Canada Inc., Toronto
Prentice-Hall of India Private Limited, New Delhi
Prentice-Hall of Japan, Inc., Tokyo
Prentice-Hall of Southeast Asia Pte. Ltd., Singapore
Whitehall Books Limited, Wellington, New Zealand
Editora Prentice-Hall do Brasil Ltda., Rio de Janeiro

Contents

Preface

When I first became involved with the preparation of annual reports to stockholders as a financial executive and later as a professional certified public accountant, I often wondered whether the average reader understood and appreciated the information furnished. Through the efforts of the accounting profession, enlightened controllers, treasurers, financial executives, and the Securities and Exchange Commission, the disclosure and interpretation of financial data improved throughout the years. As I became less involved in professional activities and had more time to devote to my personal financial affairs, I began to realize how much annual reports had improved in recent years. I started to read the annual reports as an investor, not as an accountant. There were gold nuggets of wisdom in those pages. I did not have to dig for them—the data were right on the surface for all to see, understand, and profit from.

The many books on investments, financial statement analyses, and advice to investors and traders have very little to say about using stockholders' annual reports as an investment tool. This book was written to fill the gap and to help you understand the wealth of information sent to you each year by the management of your companies.

Most books cover the waterfront—a little bit of each of the many phases of investing, technical and nontechnical. Most books on investing are written by analysts, stockbrokers, investment advisors, financial underwriters, bankers, and other persons engaged daily in Wall Street activities. This book, written by a nonprofessional investor, takes one important investment subject and, with a minimum of technical jargon, explains it so that the average person can use the knowledge, together with other information, for successful, profitable investing.

Most books refer to the annual report merely as one of the sources of investors' information. This book describes the information included in a report, explains what each section is about, and tells what is important and what is window dressing. It helps you interpret and understand financial data by direct reference to the key ratios reported.

In a case study, it takes you step by step through the annual report of a major company to show you how each part contributes to your knowledge of the company.

In the discussion of the auditor's report it shows you how to recognize an early warning signal. Such a variation from the normal report saves some stockholders substantial sums because they recognize future financial disasters.

Use this book as a handy investment guide. When you are flooded with many annual reports, the knowledge gained from this volume will be a great timesaver. As you become proficient in examining reports, the time you spend on each becomes less and the knowledge you gain about your company becomes more.

This project was discussed with a number of people whose kind words, assistance, and encouragement are acknowledged. Among them are partners of my former firm, customers' representatives of several major stock brokerages, members of the Y's Men (a retired-men's club in Westport, Connecticut) who were investors, and others too numerous to mention.

Last but not least, I want to thank the typing pool and reproduction staff of Alexander Grant & Company, who transcribed, typed, and produced the manuscript, and my loving wife, Diana, who, as always, encouraged me, aided me with my correspondence, and was very patient while I researched and wrote this book.

Annual reports
Come glossy and slick—
Especially when earnings
Are spindly and sick.

ROBERT GORDON

1

Introduction

When you first purchased marketable securities you started a business, the business of investments, which should be operated the same as any other business activity that you might enter into. The practice of investing in stocks, bonds, stock options, commodity trades, or any form of investment is a business having most of the attributes of any commercial activity.

First consider how much capital you want to invest. Then budget your expenditures. Establish objectives and goals and plan accordingly. You should provide for a flow of information so that you can make sound business and financial judgments. You should take inventory periodically, perhaps once every quarter but at least once a year, to determine the value of the investments and whether your purchases and earnings are reaching the goals and objectives you had established.

It is the objective of this book to enlighten you upon the use of one of the most valuable sources of information for accomplishing the objectives and goals of your entrepreneurial enterprise of investing—the annual stockholders' report (also called the shareholders' report) of the corporations in which you have made investments or in which you intend to invest.

OBJECTIVE OF THE INVESTMENT BUSINESS

The objective of the investment business is to make money through profits from the purchase and sales of securities and from interest and dividends.

Initially you should consider what your basic goals are, what the results of the investments are to be used for, and where you want to be five, ten, fifteen or more years hence. You must consider your financial, social, and economic positions before you start. What regular income do you have and how much of it do you need for your lifestyle? What problems will you face if you lose all the money you plan to invest? What financial risks are you willing to take? Should you deal in highly speculative situations where the risk is great but where the potential gain is also great? You can compare this with the conservative approach where the risk is low and the gains are possible slow. You will probably end up somewhere between these two extremes. You should also consider how much income you need from these investments, dividends, interest, or capital gains. Can you reinvest these increments or do you need them for current living expenses?

If you are a young single person just starting out in the financial and business world, you can afford to take risks entirely different from those of a person just getting married or a person about to retire after a full life of productive work. This is all part of general planning for establishing your investment business budget. How much do you want to invest now? What investments should you make? How much can you invest from normal earnings during future periods?

You should also determine how much time you are willing and able to spend in study, research, and investigation of the vast amount of literature available. How will you study the industries that interest you? How will you study each company you are considering investing in? There should be a reason for each purchase, an anticipated goal that can be changed as circumstances change.

THE BIG M'S

There are six major subjects to consider when evaluating a company for investment purposes. They are:

- Management experience and capabilities
- Money as reported in financial statements

- Materials used for production and merchandise held for sale
- Machinery, plant, and equipment
- Marketing of products or services
- Market price of securities

Management

A successful company usually has good management, experienced in its field and in other fields of endeavor. Top management is the board of directors and the company's elected officers. Good management instills confidence in the company and its ability to use the assets at its disposal for the growth and profits that are usually reflected in the bottom line—the earnings per share. High confidence in management's ability to enhance the value of the security is often reflected in the market price for the stock.

The board of directors manages by establishing policies to be administered by the officers they elect to run the company on a day-to-day basis. Management also includes a large body of personnel hired by the officers to perform under the policies established by the board and the direction established by the officers. This team works hard to improve earnings for and increase the value of your investment. It is the most important asset of your company.

Money as Reported in Financial Statements

When a company begins business it obtains money from the stockholders, who, in turn, receive shares of stock representing their pro rata interest in the company's earnings and assets. This money purchases assets, pays organizational expenses, and gives the corporation the financing required to run the business. As time progresses, additional money is instilled either through retention of earnings, borrowings, and additional issuances of securities. The money situation is constantly reported by financial statements to the stockholders and by many kinds of accounting reports to management for determining the progress that is being made and for making decisions.

From the investor's viewpoint, the financial statements in the annual report consist of the following:

- The statement of earnings reporting the results of the business operations for the period under review.
- The balance sheet, which reports the assets or property owned by the company (which is separate and distinct from the owners, i.e., stockholders) and the debts of the corporate enterprise as of a date. It includes

the book value of the stockholders' equity.[1] It is called a "balance sheet" because the total of the assets is the same amount of dollars as the total of the liabilities plus the stockholders' equity. These final total numbers are meaningless and are just an accountant's means to satisfy himself that to some extent the accounts are properly recorded.

- Most companies include a statement of changes in stockholders' equity showing the transactions in these accounts during the year under review. If there is no such statement, the few changes can be summarized in the notes to the financial statements.

- Another statement of significance is the Statement of Changes in Financial Position, sometimes referred to as a Fund Statement. It reports the sources of funds, in essence adjusting the net income to increases and decreases of funds for noncash items, reflecting the net increase or decrease in funds or working capital. The statement then shows the amounts that the working capital structure increased and decreased.

As an integral part of the financial statements, all companies include Notes to the Financial Statements that are explanatory and enable the reader to better understand the amounts that have been reported.

Each of these financial statements will be discussed in further detail later in this book.

Materials Used for Production and Merchandise Held for Sale

A corporation that sells a product must maintain a stock in trade, just as a corner grocery must. In a manufacturing industry the time lag from the purchase of the raw material to the sale of the finished goods may vary greatly depending upon the nature of the process. Such companies may require a tremendous investment in inventories. Companies that do not manufacture but buy finished products for resale must maintain sufficient stock so that they can promptly and effectively meet the demands of the marketplace. The management of inventory is a highly skilled technique. The term used about the ability of a company to be successful inventory managers is *the rapidity of the turnover* of their inventory. Each turnover from the acquisition of the product to the sale and collection includes a profit that enables the company to grow and expand. Management of inventories is related to the marketing concept and is sometimes discussed in the management's report. If the inventory of a company in relation to its revenues shows an increase, there is a question as to whether too much of the company's finances is tied up in slow-moving or stagnant inventory. If so, this is a danger signal. That message should alert the investor.

[1]See Chapter 13, page 111.

Machinery, Plant, and Equipment

In some companies, particularly a company that furnishes services rather than products, the issue of machinery, plants, and equipment is not a very significant item. However, every company must have some physical assets to enable it to perform. Different industries have different degrees of requirements. A capital-intensive company is one that requires tremendous amounts of money for fixed assets to perform its functions. Such industries are public utilities, manufacturing of heavy steel, manufacturing of automobiles, processing of industrial chemicals, and so on, whereas companies that perform a service need not invest a great amount of money in such tangible assets.

Marketing of Products or Services

A company must convince the public—its customers, corporate or individuals—that its product or services are highly desirable and thereby create the lifeblood of the business, a flow of funds to continue the cycle of obtaining additional products or services for sale to customers. This function is an important one, thus the reader of annual reports should examine the extent to which the corporation discusses its marketing programs.

Market Price of Securities

Investments are initially made with the thought that the market price will go up. This, plus the current dividend received by the investor, is what investing is all about. There are many matters that have a bearing on the movement of stock prices. There are the obvious ones, such as change in the earnings, which is reflected in the price/earnings ratio; current dividends and current percentage yield, which are all shown in the daily report of stock transactions and market prices; sometimes the book value of the security as reflected on the balance sheet of the company is reflected in the market price; however, many companies of solid reputation have the stock selling at prices below the book value. Other companies may be selling as much as two, three, or more times the book value. This is based upon how the marketplace assesses the value and the future prospects of the company. This relationship should be examined very closely by the investor. These matters can be discerned in part by reading annual reports.

In addition to the many internal influences upon the market price of a stock, there are many external matters, such as the prices of all stocks generally, whether a stock is in a favored industry, rumors of all sorts, the state of the economy, and so on. It is not my intention to discuss these. I will deal only with understanding annual reports and how they can help make investment decisions.

Each of the big M's will be discussed throughout the book at the appropriate time. The importance of each to an individual stockholder depends to some extent upon the purpose of the investment and the goal established when the stock was purchased. However, these might change, and every security should be examined periodically, giving appropriate weight to each of the six M's as determined by the importance in the particular industry in which your investment is operating.

Before you go any further, obtain the last annual report of the company that is your favorite investment. Skim through it, looking for each of the big M's. As you read the chapter pertaining to each M, read that portion of the report, following the suggestions I make. You will discover how much more meaningful that part of the report becomes. When you finish reading this book together with the annual report, you will find that you know a lot more about your company than when you started. That knowledge will help you make better decisions.

SOURCES FOR INVESTMENT INFORMATION

An investor should not invest on the basis of the annual report alone. There are many other sources available. Ther are many books about the security markets and how they operate, books on investing, get-rich-quick books, and so on that can be bought or borrowed from a library. Stockbrokers willingly furnish customers and potential customers with publications about industries, companies, market conditions, and recommendations.

There are many investment services that publish newsletters, analyze securities and make recommendations. Some are one-man operations; some are merely tip sheets that advertise their good and successful recommendations; others are large and independent, and a few large ones are subsidiaries of major corporations. All are required to register with the Securities and Exchange Commission (SEC). The services and cost vary considerably. These publications can be examined in the public libraries or at a broker's office and are a good souce of up-to-date information.

Several business-oriented magazines are good reading, a means for keeping informed about the business world. They are excellent sources for current newsworthy events about public and private companies. Subscribe to at least one.

Major newspapers in large cities have excellent daily business sections. In addition, *The Wall Street Journal* is published daily on a national basis and is a must for anyone who is an investor or trader in marketable securities.

Last but not least are the annual reports and the related proxy statement issued by publicly owned companies.

WHAT THIS BOOK IS ALL ABOUT

This book describes the annual report and specifically is designed to give you information on how to take advantage of the material that is furnished by the corporation in its annual reports to stockholders. It will identify important information for investment decision making as distinguished from interesting but nonimportant matters that fill many pages of the average annual report. This is a subject that is not discussed in other books on investments.

Companies that have issued voting stock to the public are required to send an annual report to stockholders as part of the proxy solicitation process. This document may consist of anything from twenty to seventy pages of interesting facts, pictures, discussions, and data, depending upon the size of the company and how much public relations and advertising material it wants to include. Much of this material is useful, but it takes much time to read, understand, and analyze it.

This book will describe how these documents are prepared, what usually is in them, and how to select the real golden nuggets of information from all the data furnished. A report can give you insight in the management of the company by the way it describes how it is operating "your company" (an oft-used phrase). Remember that these reports are frequently the product of a public relations staff and its consultants. The reports are usually beautiful examples of the printers' art, with pretty pictures and glowing reports by management of its successes and what the future has in store.

I will tell you how to evaluate all this data in light of your objectives and goals.

Bear in mind that stockholders' reports are not always the most timely of documents. The information contained usually is relevant as of the end of the fiscal year (most companies report as of December 31) and of the results of operations for the period then ended. The earliest that reports for December 31 reporting corporations are received is usually the first or second week in February. However, most reports are issued during March or in early April. Much can happen between the time the report material is completed and you get it. Therefore, investors should not base their judgment on annual reports alone but should use other material from more current sources. They should be read in relation to the objectives initially established for each security to evaluate progress and whether the company still meets original objectives and goals. Look for changes and circumstances that might change your opinion of the company and the investment. Use the annual report as part of the periodic inventory of testing the value of securities held, to determine whether you want to buy more, continue to hold, or to sell. Remember that the annual shareholders' report and the related proxy statement together with the Form 10-K filed with the Securities and Exchange Commission is the most complete information that is received by the stockholders.

HOW TO PROCEED

Don't read this book from beginning to end; there may be some chapters that are of little or no interest to you. Some can be overlooked; others need only be scanned. In others select only those areas that interest you. Read this book in the sequence of your interests. Some chapters should be read several times to get full value from them. This book should be read with the same selectivity as, I hope, with which one reads annual reports. Indeed, annual reports themselves should not be read from cover to cover except by a deeply committed student of such financial material.

2

The Tools for Personal Investment Management

There are few subjects that are written about as thoroughly as that of investments and the stock market. An investor, whether a beginner or one who is experienced and has a high degree of sophistication, should take advantage of this available printed knowledge. Public libraries have many books that will add to your sophistication as an investor. There are some excellent inexpensive paperbacks and some very expensive technical books on financial analysis. Find what serves your purpose best, and read it and study it. If you find a good book, buy a copy for your personal reference library.

HOW TO START

For the beginner, it is worthwhile to discuss your proposed program with a stockbroker. Visit several of them in their offices and determine whether they can serve your needs. Find out what literature they have available and will furnish to you, in most cases at no cost. It is particularly advisable to learn about the industries in which you desire to invest. Before selecting individual stocks, get to know something about those industries. It is advisable to select only a few industries that meet your specific needs. There are styles in investing, just as there are styles in clothing, automobiles, and housing. At one time, public utilities were in great demand; another time, the electronic industries; then high-tech companies; for a few years, conglomerates were popular. Make a selection of those industries suited for investment based upon your background and experience, knowledge and understanding, even if limited. A little knowledge is better than none.

To go one step further, you should know something about the company in which you want to invest before making the purchase. For this purpose, one of the most valuable sources of information is one that you can get free of charge, the annual stockholders' report. You might be able to get a copy of the annual report from your broker. If not, a phone call or a letter to the company will quickly bring it to you. If requested, they will send you the annual report, the proxy statement, and a copy of Form 10-K (or its equivalent) as filed with the SEC.

The purpose here is to enlighten you as to how to use this literature without reading all the material that is included; how to select those matters that most interest you about the company; to either confirm your judgment or to warn you about the possibility of trouble. But as an investor you should not live by the stockholders' annual reports alone. There are many other souces of valuable information that are more current than the information you get in the annual report prepared by the company. The report for the company is usually issued about forty-five days after the close of the fiscal year and sometimes as late as six months. Many things can happen during that interim period.

READING MATERIALS

The following section lists some periodicals and sources that are available.

Brokers' Information

The broker you select undoubtedly will have a great number of brochures, pamphlets, newsletters, and other periodicals that can be furnished on a regular basis or at request. Take advantage of this; you're paying for it in the commissions you pay every time you make a purchase or sale. This information is prepared by the brokerage firm's research department, is current, and often includes an analysis of companies and their securities.

Customer representatives make it their business to follow the affairs of a number of companies, attending stockholders' meetings, visiting the companies, and talking with their top officials. The representatives can make suggestions and recommendations for investments based upon their studies and research. Take advantage of this service. It's invaluable.

Daily Newspapers

It is a must to read the financial section of the daily newspaper. In some cities there are major newspapers that have reasonably good financial pages giving newsworthy information about companies in their geographical area or nationally in addition to the daily stock prices. One newspaper that is national in scope is published daily from coast to coast and has the best daily news for investors—*The Wall Street Journal*. Copies can be purchased at newsstands; a subscription is reasonably priced for daily mail delivery.

Another newspaper has been expanding its financial news daily on a national basis; it is the *New York Times*. In terms of financial reporting it is not as complete as *The Wall Street Journal*, but if you live in the normal distribution area of the *Times* it will be worth your while to make it part of your daily reading. If there is important news with regard to a stock exchange–listed company or a major over-the-counter company, you can be sure that it will be in the *New York Times*, though not always covered as completely as in *The Wall Street Journal*.

If you live near a major city, you will find that the local newspapers will serve your purpose. In smaller cities, local papers generally publish news related to companies in their geographical distribution area. This might suggest that it is not a bad idea to confine your investments to companies within that geographical area plus some major national companies who may have local divisions or operations.

Magazines and Other Periodicals

There are weekly, biweekly, and monthly magazines published for the investing public. Some are highly technical, some are very newsy, some are written in a style easy to read, some are very businesslike and full of jargon. Find one or two that serve your purpose and are easy to read and understand. It is well worth the subscription price for the story behind the story in the newspaper.

Investment Services

There are a host of subscription services for investment information or recommendations. Some may be called "tip sheets" that recommend the purchase of specific securities. Many of these advertise regularly in the financial pages of newspapers. The prices range from modest amounts to the very expensive; the latter are geared toward the analyst and the professional investor, the former toward the nonprofessional. Most brokerage firms subscribe to and have loose-leaf services in their office, such as Standard & Poor's, Moody's or Value Line that report on many companies, revising and updating the information, keeping it current. If you want to find out about any company, the broker can send you a photocopy of a one-page summary from one of these services. It is worthwhile to investigate some of the services that are within an affordable price range depending upon the size of your investment portfolio.

Most public libraries subscribe to Standard & Poor's, Moody's, Value Line, and other popular services. It is worth spending a few hours a month in the public library going through these, examining the most current information pertaining to the securities you own or are interested in.

THE ANNUAL REPORT

The annual stockholders' report, the proxy statement, and Form 10-K of each company will be described later in this book. at this point it need only be said that this report is a source of basic information that is invaluable in trying to decide whether you should buy a security and, if you own it, whether you should retain it or whether you should sell it. It also is a source for determining whether you should increase or reduce your holdings

One of the best ways to increase your holdings is to subscribe to the dividend reinvestment plan that many companies provide for their stockholders. Each quarterly dividend is reinvested in the number of shares, including fractions, that the amount of the dividend will purchase at the current market price, or in some instances at a small discount. Some companies do not charge brokers' fees or any service charge; others have a nominal service charge. This is a bargain. It also conforms with the price averaging investment program that many financial advisors recommend as a means of establishing and building up a portfolio where a fixed amount is invested each month, quarter year, or year in companies, thereby averaging prices over a long period of time.

ANNUAL STOCKHOLDERS' MEETING

If you have sufficient time, attend the annual stockholders' meeting. It is an excellent source of information. It will give you an opportunity to observe members of management during the meeting as they present prepared statements and deal with questions from the floor. The most valuable knowledge obtained is from the questions asked by the stockholders and the replies. Most of those that ask questions are usually quite knowledgeable about the company's operations and therefore make very keen and interesting inquiries.

Most of these meetings last only a few hours. Try to attend them, especially if they are held in your area.

SUMMARY

To invest successfully and to avoid losses requires knowledge of your investment business. Keep informed, using as many tools that your available time permits. You will find that the time is well spent and can result in a pleasurable and profitable experience.

3

How Stockholders'
Annual Reports Developed

WHAT THE ANNUAL REPORT IS

Annual reports are issued in great profusion to stockholders of publicly held companies.[1] The printed report can be a simple four-page black-and-white document stating the minimum amount of information required by the SEC, or it can be a beautiful multi-colored booklet of thirty-six or more pages.

Just what is it? What are its objectives? Is it an advertising medium, a publicity brochure, a beautiful sample of the printer's and engraver's art? Is it a document extolling the virtues and successes of management? Does it represent an ego trip for the chief executive officer of the corporation? Is it a report to stockholders of management's performance so that the stockholder can evaluate what has happened in the recent past and equate that with what the future may hold? Is it an investment tool whereby the stockholder can decide whether to buy more shares of stock of the company, sell all or part of his present stock, or hold his present stock position?

[1]This chapter is taken in part from *Working with the Public Accountant—a Guide for Managers at All Levels.* © Adolph G. Lurie, published by McGraw-Hill Book Company, 1977.

In most instances, the annual report is not limited to reporting past events to stockholders but has multiple uses of investment value. Depending upon the reporting company and the investor-reader, it can be one or it can be several or all of the above. If you know what to look for, an annual report can be very enlightening. Here you will learn how to separate the meaningful information from the window dressing.

The report of a research project sponsored by the Financial Executives Research Foundation and conducted by Booz, Allen & Hamilton, Inc., in 1973 on "The Businessman's View of the Purposes of Financial Reporting"[2] included the following partial summary of its key findings on the question "From management's viewpoint, what are the purposes of published financial reports?"

1. Accounting for performance, or financial stewardship in behalf of the owners, is the primary purpose cited for financial reporting.
2. Published financial statements are considered to be only one part of an overall reporting environment; *management views its reporting responsibilities as transcending the capabilities of accounting.* [Emphasis not in original.]
3. The primary purpose of published financial reports, per se, is the measurement of past performance.
4. A second, a far less important, purpose cited was that financial statements indicate investment quality.

Since the question referred to published financial reports, a conclusion was stated that "supplemental text is required to further document the quality of stewardship to date." In other words, there is much more than numbers in the report to help you decide whether your investment meets your financial purposes and goals.

HOW ANNUAL REPORTS EVOLVED

In early years of publicly owned corporate enterprises very little information was submitted to stockholders. There was no compulsion to issue annual reports until the stock exchanges included that requirement in listing agreements. However, details of form and content were not specified. Accordingly, the management of some companies believed that it was inappropriate to disclose much information to stockholders because annual reports would be read by competitors who then could make important decisions and thereby become more com-

[2]Copyright © 1973 The Financial Executives Research Foundation.

petitive. Some companies would not show net sales or revenues in the earnings statement but would report gross earnings from sales and show a few other items, such as selling and administrative expenses, interest, and taxes, and arrive at the net profit figure.

Reports often consisted merely of one sheet of four pages, with a summarized statement of earnings, a condensed balance sheet, a surplus statement, and a brief letter from the president saying, in effect, "Here it is. We did well." Enlightened companies, of course, issued more detailed statements.

When the Securities and Exchange Commission was established in 1933, it began the trend toward more disclosure of information for stockholders. Rules were established that influenced the information that was included in the annual reports of companies whose securities are held by the public and registered with the SEC. However, the SEC does not directly monitor the information reported in the financial statements.

The SEC does, however, have the responsibility of monitoring the *form* and *content* of proxy statements sent to stockholders for the annual stockholders' meeting. It requires that an annual report, as part of the proxy statement, be sent with or before the proxy statements. Thus the SEC becomes involved in the contents of and the disclosures in the financial report. In order to accomplish its task the SEC requires companies to file an annual report on Form 10-K that includes the financial data and other additional information.

During the early 1930s, there was a movement toward simplification of the financial statements that were included in the annual report. Efforts were made to enable the average stockholder to be able to read and understand the statement of earnings, balance sheet, and statement of retained earnings, the only financial statements required at that time. The balance sheet format was sometimes submitted as a statement of financial position whereby current liabilities were deducted from current assets to reflect net working capital, and the noncurrent assets less noncurrent liabilities were added thereto to reflect the net worth of the company. This was balanced with a statement of the composition of net worth—that is, equity securities plus donated capital and retained earnings. The captions were usually in simple language such as "This is what we own" and "This is what we owe." However, this attempt to simplify annual reports never really took off.

According to the SEC, the name of the game is disclosure. It became difficult to meet the disclosure requirements by simplified language and simplified reports. Because of litigation started by stockholders, the legal profession got into the act to see that the correct "*t*'s" were crossed and the correct "*i*'s" dotted.

Regulation S-X of the SEC established the form and content of financial statements. Modifications and changes in reporting are made from time to time through the issuance of Accounting Series Releases, which touch upon any subject that pertains to accounting, financial reporting, proxy statements, amendments to rules, regulations, or other releases. There were 297 such releases issued up to September 1981, some important but many of minor significance. Major additional disclosure requirements were added by the issuance of guidelines for reports for the years ended December 31, 1974, and thereafter.

Effective for fiscal years ending after March 15, 1978, the SEC adopted a new integrated disclosure regulation, Regulation S-K, amending certain disclosure forms and rules to integrate the information presented in annual reports, proxys, and the annual report to the SEC on Form 10-K, among others. The more important changes and additional changes were:

- Description of general development of the business during the prior five years
- Financial information about business segments, i.e. grouping the company's products and services by principal industries and businesses
- Narrative description of business
- Financial information about foreign and domestic operations
- Sample disclosure statements are set forth
- Description of property (land, buildings, natural resources, machinery, equipment, etc.)
- Identification of directors
- Management remuneration
- Security ownership of certain beneficial owners and management
- Market prices of the common stock
- Management's discussion and analysis of financial condition and result of operations
- Supplementary financial information.

Some of these represented expansion of existing requirements and others were added; some apply to the annual report and proxy statement, and some apply to Form 10-K. As previously stated, a copy of Form 10-K can be obtained from the company at no cost. It is good reading.

Most companies print a large quantity of annual reports, more than two or three times the number of registered stockholders, and distribute the report widely. Sufficient copies are sent to stockbrokers to send to their customers who own stock but retain the certificates in street name (that is, in the name of a broker or nominee). The companies also send copies to brokers, analysts, bankers, underwriters, insurance companies, and many others who want them for information, for analyses, and for their files. In addition, requests are made by instructors, scholars, and many others for investment purposes and for research and study, and by nonstockholders who have varying interests in the company.

WHO READS THE ANNUAL STOCKHOLDERS' REPORT?

By its title, it would appear that the annual report is written for and addressed to the company's stockholders. The president's letter is addressed to the stockholders. The auditor's report is most frequently addressed to the board of directors and stockholders, although sometimes only to the board of directors or other times only to the stockholders. However, the textual material is usually written with a much wider audience in mind.

The Financial Executives Research Foundation in its 1973 project inquired of major executives, "Who are the principal audiences for established financial statements, and what is the relative importance of each?" Its key findings, which apply only to the financial statements in the annual report, were:

1. Ninety percent of companies interviewed accord the present stockholder top priority in financial reporting.
2. The second most important audience was described as "the financial community," including security analysts, financial "opinion makers," potential shareholders, or others in positions to affect decisions to buy, hold, or sell securities.
3. Corporate executives have strongly mixed feelings toward security analysts, but most believe that as a practical matter they are a powerful influence, particularly in the short term, as evidenced by the fact that institutions in 1971 accounted for ownership of 18 percent of New York Stock Exchange-listed stocks but accounted for about 70 percent of NYSE trading volume.
4. No other audience was accorded nearly the importance of those noted above.

Arthur Andersen & Co., one of the nation's major accounting firms, commissioned Opinion Research Corporation in 1974 to conduct a comprehensive, completely independent survey that resulted in a report issued in December 1974 entitled "Public Accounting in Transition."[3] The survey involved 404 individual shareholders interviewed by telephone and 457 key publics interviewed in depth. The key publics were:

[3]Copyright 1974, Arthur Andersen & Co.

Corporate executive	262
Investment analysts and brokers	34
Institutional investors and portfolio managers	31
Accountants	30
Securities lawyers	27
Others (professors, press, government officials, etc.)	73
Total key publics	457

The replies from key publics concerning whom the annual reports should be written for were:

Sophisticated investors	8%
Average investors	33%
Both	58%
Other	1%
Total	100%

This question was not asked of shareowners. Instead, the query concerning attention given to the annual report was "Do you read all of it, most of it, or don't you read it at all?" The results were:

Read all of it	36%
Read most of it	36%
Just glance at it	24%
Don't read it	4%
Total	100%

Two further questions were asked about how often the stockholders read the financial statements and how often they read the auditor's report. The results reported were:

	Read Financial Statements	Read Auditor's Report
All of the time	38%	19%
Most of the time	34%	31%
Only sometimes	16%	28%
Rarely or never	11%	21%
No response	1%	1%
Total	100%	100%

These reponses would seem to dispel the common notion that stockholders do not generally read annual reports. However, I wonder what the answers would have been if the questions pertained to the present expanded version of the annual reports.

THE INFLUENCE OF THE INDEPENDENT AUDITOR

Independent certified public accountants have created a high degree of confidence in the financial statements and their report thereon by establishing rules, regulations, and standards enforceable through their professional society, the American Institute of Certified Public Accountants (AICPA), and its ethics committee.

The SEC requires that the financial statements in the annual report (and in most other filings) must be examined by independent professional auditors who are certified public accountants. The examinations are made in accordance with generally accepted auditing standards (GAAS). These standards are a set of rules and procedures as prescribed by the AICPA.

Prior to the first issuance of audit standards, the American Institute of Accountants, now the AICPA, in 1917, at the request of the Federal Trade Commission, prepared a memorandum on balance sheet audits, which was published by the Federal Reserve Board. In 1929, the AICPA established a committee to revise the memorandum and issue pamphlets. This committee and its successors were active throughout the following years. In 1939, the Committee on Auditing Procedures was formed to examine auditing procedures and related questions. In 1947, it issued a tentative statement of auditing standards (as distinguished from auditing procedures). Since then these standards have grown into a substantial set of rules, codified in 1972 (a 235-page book) by the Auditing Standards Executive Committee, now called the Auditing Standards Board. Since then these standards have been updated by thirty-nine statements on Auditing Standards as changed circumstances required.

The standards are as follows:

- The General Standards
    Training and proficiency
    Independence
    Due care with performance of work
- The Standards of Field Work
    Adequacy of planning and timing
    Study and evaluation of internal control
    Evidential matter (working papers)
- Standards of Reporting (audit reports)
    Adherence to Generally Accepted Accounting
        Principles (GAAP)
    Consistency of application of GAAP
    Adequacy of informative disclosure
    Expression of opinion in the auditors' report

      i. Unqualified opinion
     ii. Qualified opinion
   iii. Adverse opinion
   iv. Unaudited financial statements
- Other types of reports

The standards of reporting refers to the brief statements—usually one, two, or three paragraphs—accompanying the financial statements and signed by the auditor. It is usually identified as "Report of Independent Certified Public Accountant" or by a similar title and will be discussed more fully in Chapter 4. Because of its importance, the development, meaning, and significance of generally accepted accounting principles are also discussed in Chapter 4.

It can be readily seen that the accounting profession has been keeping up with the times, the demands of the SEC, the information needs of the investing public, the desire to improve the quality of financial reporting by companies, and the enhancement of public confidence in financial reporting.

In spite of these efforts, there has been a cloud over the CPA profession resulting from a series of disclosures in the 1960s and 1970s of corruption in major corporations involving alleged fraudulent financial statements, bribes, kickbacks, and corporate failures resulting from fraud, misfeasance, malfeasance, and nonfeasance. These often were perpetrated by employees, officers, management, and others and resulted, in some instances, in serious losses by stockholders. In many situations, the independent auditors as well as the stockholders were the victims. However, the resulting litigation was directed against the management and the auditors, the latter particularly for failure to discover and disclose the problem.

THE METCALF REPORT: THE ACCOUNTING ESTABLISHMENT

The federal government got into the act in 1975 with a staff study prepared by the Subcommittee on Reports, Accounting, and Mangement of the Committee on Government Operations. The report was entitled "The Accounting Establishment" and has been referred to as the Metcalf report after the committee chairman, Senator Lee Metcalf of Montana. It was dated December 7, 1976, and ordered to be printed on March 31, 1977, as a paperback of 1,760 pages. It was 2½ inches thick and very critical of the accounting profession.

The principal recommendations were:

1. Congress should exercise stronger oversight of accounting practices promulgated or approved by the federal government and more leadership in establishing proper goals and policies.
2. Congress should establish comprehensive accounting objectives for the federal government to guide agencies and departments in performing their responsibilities.
3. Congress should amend the federal securities laws to restore the rights of damaged individuals to sue independent auditors for negligence under the fraud provisions of the securities laws.
4. Congress should consider methods of increasing competition among accounting firms.
5. The federal government should directly establish financial accounting standards for publicly owned companies.
6. The federal government should establish auditing standards used by independent auditors to certify the accuracy of corporate financial statements and supporting records.

These are the first six of fifteen recommendations. It is evident that the Metcalf report created a tremendous hue and cry from the accounting profession, the financial world, and corporate management. If these recommendations were accepted, these groups felt, the federal government would regulate business and the investment world.

SELF-REGULATION PROCEDURES

The accounting profession, through the AICPA, its national organization, has been studying means to improve its self-regulation procedures. It has been encouraged by the SEC to take appropriate steps.

Prior to September 1977, the AICPA was a professional organization of individual members and was not structured to regulate the activities of CPA firms. In September 1977, the council of the AICPA established the Division fo CPA Firms, comprising an SEC Practice Section and a Private Companies Practice Section, to implement a program of voluntary self-regulation and self-disciplining of the profession and created the authority to sanction member firms for failure to comply with established requirements for practice.

The key objectives of the SEC section were:

1. To improve the quality of accounting and auditing practice by establishing practice requirements.

2. To establish and maintain an effective system of self-regulation of member firms by means of mandatory triannual peer reviews of a firm's accounting and auditing practice, required maintenance of an appropriate system of quality control, and the imposition of sanctions for failure to meet membership requirements or for major deficiencies revealed by the peer review process.

In its bylaws, the SEC Practice Section provided for a Public Oversight Board (POB) to enhance the effectiveness of the system. The POB consists of five members, prominent individuals of high integrity and reputation. The initial board included no CPAs.

The peer review program is administered by a Peer Review Committee of fifteen individuals from member firms. Peer reviews are performed by member firms or by competent individual members of the AICPA selected by the Peer Review Committee.

The POB employs a full-time staff of highly qualified CPAs and when required may hire temporary part-time retired CPA firm partners to supplement the permanent staff. The staff monitors the activities of the Peer Review Committee by a selection process of reviews made by the SEC section. Detailed procedures have been promulgated to deal with deviations from established standards.

This limited discussion relates to the SEC section activities pertaining to public companies. Other monitoring procedures are not pertinent to the readers of this book.

Although the self-regulating procedure is relatively new, it appears to be functioning satisfactorily. The monitoring activities of the POB are reviewed by the SEC, and it has issued favorable comments. With so many watchdogs around there is every reason to believe that major auditing firms are doing what is necessary to avoid both the bark and the bite of the Metcalf Committee.

A WORD OF CAUTION

Beware! In spite of all the self-regulation, a serious loss can occur by fraud undetected by the most experienced and expert CPA. A brilliant management with fraudulent intent can fool the most knowledgeable independent professional auditor by shrewd maneuvering of paperwork and records and by collusive effort with the intent to deceive, manipulate, and defraud. Even with sophisticated computers and well-trained internal auditors, these deeds can be done. Even government regulations cannot stop it. All this can be observed in the fraudulent failures of the past—such as those of Equity Funding Corp., National Students Marketing Corp., Continental Vending Machine Corp., Sterling Homex Corp., United Brands Co., to mention just a few.

The procedures that have been established make it more difficult to defraud, but it still can be done. However, we can be grateful for the high degree of integrity of the management of American industry, commerce, and finance and that of independent certified public accountants.

4

The Auditors'
Report Letter

THE STANDARD REPORT

If you look carefully, you will find a one-, two-, or three-paragraph item among the financial statements with a heading reading "Auditors' Opinion," "Report of Independent Auditors," "Report of Independent Certified Public Accountant," or similar words.[1] The standard report reads as follows:

> We have examined the balance sheets of the XYZ Corp. as of June 30, 1983 and June 30, 1982, and the related statements of operations, accumulated earnings and changes in financial position for the year then ended. Our examination was made in accordance with generally accepted auditing standards and, accordingly, included such tests of the accounting records and such other auditing procedures as we considered necessary in the circumstances.

> In our opinion, the financial statements referred to above present fairly the financial position of the XYZ Corp. at June 30, 1983 and June 30, 1982 and the results of their operations and changes in financial position for the year then ended, in conformity with generally accepted accounting principles applied on a consistent basis.

[1]This chapter is taken in part from *Working with the Public Accountant—a Guide for Managers at All Levels.* © Adolph G. Lurie, published by McGraw-Hill Book Company, 1977. It includes reporting requirements established since 1977.

This is one of the most important statements in the annual report.

The first paragraph, usually called the "scope" paragraph, tells what has been done. The last paragraph, called "the opinion," is what the company expects to get if everything is all right.

There are three types of variations. A third paragraph that follows the scope is usually an explantion. Read it carefully. The explanation may result in the disclaimer of opinion, an adverse opinion, or a qualified opinion in the final paragraph. Also, look for a phrase beginning with "subject to . . ." or "except that . . ." in the opinion paragraph. It usually is placed within the paragraph, not at the beginning or the end.

If either of these occurs, look out. They usually mean trouble. Read them carefully. They might refer to further comments in the "Notes to Financial Statements." Read that carefully also. Then form your own conclusion about the significance of the disclosure and the impact it might have.

There is a more detailed discussion of disclaimer and adverse and qualified opinions later in this chapter. After you have become familiar with the standard opinion, the opinion in each annual report need not be read. They are all more or less alike. The only time that you should read the auditors' opinion is when there is a third paragraph or a qualification in the final paragraph. Either of these can be discerned by a quick glance.

SIGNIFICANCE OF THE OPINION

The following explains the meaning of the opinion and the importance that should be given to this portion of the annual report.

The only official CPA contribution to the annual report is the auditor's opinion, in which the CPA either gives an opinion that the financial statements are in conformity with generally accepted accounting principles (GAAP) applied on a basis consistent with that of the preceding year or qualifies the opinion and states the reasons therefor.

The phrase ". . . in conformity with generally accepted accounting principles . . ." contains probably the most important seven words in the auditors' opinion.

If the financial statements do not conform with generally accepted accounting principles (GAAP), the auditor is unable to give an unqualified opinion and must explain why he cannot do so. Hence anyone reading or needing to review financial statements should be aware of the significance of these seven words.

The seven words pertain only to the audited financial statements as identified in the scope paragraph. It should be understood that the financial statements are not the certified public accountants' statements but the company's statements. Anyone reading the financial statements should be aware of this important fact, even though the CPA may contribute significantly to the language of the statements and the amounts reported. This is usually stated in the "Report of the Management" or as a separate item captioned "Management Responsibility for Financial Statements" that precedes the financial statements. A clear example of this type of statement was included in the 1981 annual report of Eastman Kodak.

> Management is responsible for the preparation and integrity of the financial statements and related notes which appear on page 31 through 40. These statements have been prepared in accordance with generally accepted accounting principles.
>
> The company's accounting systems include extensive internal controls designed to provide reasonable assurance of the reliability of its financial records and the proper safeguarding and use of its assets. Such controls are based on established policies and procedures, are implemented by trained, skilled personnel with an appropriate segregation of duties, and are monitored by a comprehensive internal audit program.
>
> The financial statements have been examined by Price Waterhouse & Co., independent accountants, who were responsible for conducting their examination in accordance with generally accepted auditing standards. Their resulting report is on page 33.
>
> The Board of Directors exercises its reponsibility for these financial statements through its Audit Committee, which consists entirely of non-management Board members. The independent accountants and internal auditors have full and free access to the Audit Committee. The Audit Committee periodically meets privately with the independent accountants and the general auditor of the company as well as with management present to discuss accounting, auditing, and financial reporting matters.

THE FINANCIAL STATEMENTS

The financial statements generally consist of the following:

- The balance sheet
- The statement of income, the statement of earnings, or the statement of operations, whichever title is appropriate

- The statement of retained earnings or the statement of deficit in retained earnings, whichever title is appropriate
- The statement of changes in financial position
- The notes to financial statements.

HISTORY OF GENERALLY ACCEPTED ACCOUNTING PRINCIPLES

The accounting literature of the nineteenth century made very few references to accounting principles. The term began to be used in textbooks early in the twentieth century, but even then there was no clear indication of what these principles were or what they meant. However, the seed was planted, and the accounting principles tree started to grow.

Actually there was no great urgency to establish generally accepted accounting principles in the early years of this century, for few corporations were publicly owned, and the number of stockholders was relatively small. There were no official requirements for annual reports except those of the stock exchanges, and an auditor's opinion was appended to the financial statements only as a matter of practice. Taking a leaf from the book of its much older profession, the law, the accounting profession based its principle largely on precedent. The precedent was merely the fact that some major company had followed certain principles in the financial statements that were made public.

The beginning of federal income taxation in 1913 had some influence upon the thinking of the accountants, who paid greater attention to the need for accounting principles. In that period, educators, through the American Accounting Association, gave greater impetus to the development of principles than either commerce and industry or professional auditors.

The American Institute of Accountants (AIA) did not become involved with the problem until about 1917, when a pamphlet with the title "A Memorandum on Balance Sheet Audits" was prepared at the request of the Federal Trade Commission. The pamphlet was later reissued as "Uniform Accounting: A Tentative Proposal Submitted by the Federal Reserve Board." It is rather difficult to determine now which came first, a consideration of auditing procedures or accounting principles; However, it is evident that these two major subjects were closely related, since the pamphlet was again reissued in 1918 with the title "Approved Methods for the Preparation of Balance Sheet Statements." The lack of professional guidance for the development of financial principles was evident in the fact that there was no uniformity in the language of accountants' opinions in connection with their examination and reporting upon their clients' financial statements.

Perhaps the earliest effort of the AIA for developing uniformity in the activities of the accountants was the formation of the Committee on Terminology in 1920. During a period of about ten years this group compiled a vocabulary that was finally published under the title "Accounting Terminology." Later the committee was combined with and chosen from the members of the Committee on Accounting Procedures.

During the third decade of this century, forward-thinking members of the profession, aware that there were no authoritative accounting principles, began searching for ways of filling this gap in professional literature. In 1923, in cooperation with bankers, rules were developed for the accounting treatment of transactions subsequent to the date of the balance sheet which was approved by the AIA at its annual meeting that year.

In 1928, the AIA appointed a special committee, which during the next year issued a new and improved edition of the 1917 Federal Reserve Board bulletin. Now entitled "Verification of Financial Statements," it included a suggested form of certificate and the format for the balance sheet and profit and loss statement with appropriate textual material. This might be considered the first official involvement of the national accounting organization in creating accounting principles. The creation of the SEC in 1934 after the passage of the Securities Act of 1933 and the Securities Exchange Act of 1934 gave further impetus to the establishment of accounting principles.

In 1938 the Committee on Accounting Procedures was enlarged, and the AICPA established a research department. This was the first time that the committee included paid researchers. Previously the so-called common-law approach toward accounting principles had been accepted procedure, but in 1938 the committee started the series of Accounting Research Bulletins, the first official publications of accounting principles as we know them today.

This look at the history of accounting principles prior to 1938 shows the difficulties that the profession had in establishing the means for creating official accounting principles. Moreover, periods of suffering, conflict, and differences of opinion were not over: There were no means of enforcing the pronouncements of the committee. The acceptance of the Accounting Research Bulletins by members of the profes-sion and by commerce and industry was the only weapon that the profession then had to create a body of official accounting principles.

Accounting Research Bulletins

The Committee on Accounting Procedures continued until 1959. During that period there was a continuing turnover of members, and the pace of the Accounting Research Bulletins was increased. In the mid-1940s, Carman G. Blough, former chief accountant of the SEC, was retained as a full-time director of research of the AICPA. Blough contributed substantially to the acceptance of the activities of the AICPA, particularly of the Accounting Research Bulletins.

Accounting Research Bulletin No. 43 was issued in 1953 as a revision and restatement of the forty-two preceding individual bulletins. By 1959, eight new bulletins had been issued, and when the committee published its final report, it could look back with pride upon a total of fifty-one bulletins.

In its final report the committee stated: "Throughout the history of the Committee, its bulletins have increasingly been recognized as authoritative by the profession, by the business world, by governmental agencies and by the courts."

Accounting Principles Board

In 1959, after intensive study by a special committee, the development of accounting principles by the AICPA was restructured by the creation of the Accounting Principles Board (APB), which had essentially the same responsibilities as the former Committee on Accounting Procedures but acted in coordination with an expanded research division. Accounting research studies were prepared by the division as required to enable the APB to issue its opinions. The Council of the AICPA granted the new board the authority to issue opinions that presumably were binding upon all members of the Institute and represented authoritative accounting principles. However, there were no means of enforcing compliance. Opinion No. 1 and subsequent opinions included the following note:

> Opinions present the considered opinion of at least two-thirds of the members of the Accounting Principles Board, reached on a formal vote after examination of the subject matter.

> Except as indicated in the succeeding paragraph, the authority of the Opinions rests upon their general acceptability. While it is recognized

that general rules may be subject to exception, the burden of justifying departures from Board Opinions must be assumed by those who adopt other practices.

Throughout the existence of the Commtitee on Accounting Procedures and the succeeding Accounting Principles Board, these groups were criticized by industry and the financial community. It was stated that they consisted principally of professional accountants and educators and that insufficient weight was given to the problems of industrial accountants responsible for maintaining accounting records and for issuing financial statements.

THE INVESTMENT CREDIT CONTROVERSY

The first major test of the authority of the Accounting Principles Board occurred with the passage of the Revenue Act of 1962, which provided for the investment credit to stimulate investment in assets that would improve the employment situation by increasing production. Taxpayers were permitted a reduction in their income taxes by virtue of investment in certain depreciable assets acquired and placed in service during and after 1962.

In the past, accounting principles had usually been based upon existing forms of transactions and usage under various circumstances. However, with respect to the investment credit, there was no precedent upon which the board could form an opinion.

Problems first arose within the board, which issued Opinion No. 2 in December 1962. The opinion was passed by the required two-thirds majority. Three members announced that their firms would not follow the opinion. On January 10, 1963, the SEC issued Accounting Series Release No. 96, which differed from the APB opinion. Naturally, many public corporations decided to ignore the board's opinion and follow the alternative espoused by the SEC.

The resulting furor caused the APB to reevaluate its position and issue Opinion No. 4 in March 1964, in which the board restated the three concepts upon which the initial opinion was rendered.

The board had believed that its interpretation of the investment credit was supported by the weight of pertinent factors. However, since the authority of its opinions rested upon their general acceptability, in the light of developments since the issuance of Opinion No. 2, the board determined that its conclusions had not attained the degree of acceptability believed necessary to make the opinion effective. The

APB believed that although Opinion No. 2 should be considered preferable, the alternative method of treating the credit was also acceptable.

It is evident that the controversy concerning the investment credit did not enhance the authoritative position of the APB, particularly since there was conflict with respect to accounting principles both within and without professional organizations as well as in the board itself. However, the board survived, and opinions issued through the years until its demise in 1973 reached the impressive total of thirty-one.

THE PROBLEMS OF BUSINESS COMBINATIONS AND MERGERS

The accounting principles involved in business combinations became another *cause célébre* over the years. After World War II corporate acquisitions and mergers grew apace; most were recorded as mergers and consolidations in the early years. In 1950, an ARB entitled "Business Combinations Revisions" was issued. Changes were made and clarifications were issued in 1959, 1966, and 1970. Further amendments were made by the Financial Accounting Standards Board (FASB; see next section).

FINANCIAL ACCOUNTING STANDARDS BOARD (FASB)

Because of the many criticisms levied at the profession-dominated Accounting Principles Board, the AICPA through its board of directors in March 1971 appointed a seven-man group whose charter stated: "The main purpose of the study is to find ways for the American Institute of Certified Public Accountants to improve its function of establishing accounting principles. The study should consider how the Institute's standard-setting role can be made more responsive to the needs of those who rely on financial statements."

After less than a year's deliberation, the study group issued its recommendations, which were accepted by the general membership of the AICPA and other organizations and interested parties without any substantial changes. The recommendations included the formation of a Financial Accounting Foundation, established separately from all existing profesisonal bodies, whose principal duty would be to appoint the members of the FASB and to raise the funds for its operation. The committee proposed an FASB of seven members, each of whom would serve on a full-time basis and be fully remunerated. During their terms of office, the members of the FASB would have no other affiliations. Four of the members would be CPAs drawn from public practice; the other three would not need to hold a CPA certificate but should possess extensive experience in the financial-reporting field. The function of the FASB would be to establish standards of financial accounting and reporting. It is quite evident that a completely independent body with a broad base to study and develop financial accounting standards was contemplated.

The committee also proposed a Financial Accounting Standards Advisory Council of approximately twenty members to work closely with the FASB. The members would be appointed to serve one-year terms and be entitled to reimbursement of expenses but would not receive remuneration. They would be drawn from a variety of occupations, and not more than one-fourth should come from any single sphere of activity.

The Financial Accounting Standards Board succeeded the Accounting Principles Board on July 1, 1973. It began functioning by approving initially all existing and continuing announcements of the APB as effective unless it changed them by issuing new financial accounting standards.

The significance and authority of all prior bulletins and opinions and subsequent standards were solidified by the Rules of Conduct of the AICPA Code of Professional Ethics, which states that effective March 1, 1973:

> A member shall not express an opinion that financial statements are presented in conformity with generally accepted accounting principles if such statements contain any departure from an accounting principle promulgated by the body designated by Council to establish such principles which has a material effect on the statements taken as a whole, unless the member can demonstrate that due to unusual circumstances the financial statements would otherwise have been misleading. In such cases his report must describe the departure, the approximate effects thereof, if practicable, and the reasons why compliance with the principle would result in a misleading statement.

The published interpretations of the rule state, among other things, that the AICPA Council has designated statements by the FASB, together with Accounting Research Bulletins and APB Opinions that are not superseded by action of the FASB, as accounting principles. At last there were teeth in the ethics to enforce accounting principles.

DEPARTURES FROM GENERALLY ACCEPTED ACCOUNTING PRINCIPLES

Generally accepted accounting principles are not sacrosanct; neither is consistency. There are always times when a change from an accounting principles is appropriate, and no auditor would quarrel with the company if it can be demonstrated that a change is appropriate in the given circumstances. For example, if a company changes the nature of its operations or enters a different industry, a different accounting principle may be warranted or required. Similarly, a change in economic conditions may suggest a change in principle. Such a circumstance came about in 1973 and 1974 because of inflation. Many companies found it advisable and appropriate to change the method for the valuation of inventories from the lower of cost or market on the first-in, first-out (FIFO) to the last-in, first-out (LIFO) method. The annual reports of quite a number of public companies disclosed this change with the appropriate approval by their auditors. (See pages 83 and 89.)

WHAT THE AUDITORS' REPORT MEANS TO YOU

After looking at all the pretty pictures in the annual report, I suggest you look at the auditors' report. You can tell at an instance whether there is a variation from GAAP. If there is no third paragraph and no "subject to" or "effect of changes" in the opinion paragraph you are part of the way home. There is no variation.

The next step is to examine the opinion. If it says, "In our opinion, the aforementioned statements present fairly . . . in conformity with generally accepted accounting principles applied on a basis consistent with that of the preceding year," you can go on to the next item.

However, there is a real danger signal if there is an adverse opinion. These are few and far between in public companies. They usually follow a third-paragraph explanation. It usually means that trouble has arrived and more bad news is brewing.

The following examples pertains to a litigation matter disclosed and explained in a third paragraph, and the auditors' opinion thereon:

Disclaimer of Opinion

A disclaimer of opinion is issued when the auditor has not obtained sufficient competent evidential matter to form an opinion on the fairness of presentation of the financial statements as a whole. Assuming the litigation facts where the auditor does not have enough evidential material to form an opinion and the matter is material, the auditor may issue a disclaimer as follows:

> Because the matters described in the preceding paragraph [usually identified] enter materially into the determination of financial position, results of operations, and changes in financial position, we do not express an opinion on the financial statements referred to above.

Adverse Opinion

In the event that the evidential material about the litigation is sufficient for the auditor to form an opinion, but the auditor does not agree with the accounting treatment, he may give an adverse opinion as follows:

> Because of the materiality of the matters described in the preceding paragraph, we are of the opinion that the financial statements referred to *above do not present fairly*,[2] in conformity with generally accepted accounting principles, the financial position of X company at December 31, 1984, or the results of its operations and changes in the financial position for the year then ended.

Qualified Opinion

The qualified opinion is usually an alert about a problem area that is not as severe or material and probably could be overcome by some corrective action. It usually is preceded by "except that" or "subject to." The subject matter about the litigation is described in a third paragraph or in a note to the financial statements. If the auditor has information that would indicate that the amounts involved would not be material in relation to the size of the company, its revenue and net income and that the ultimate conclusion of the matter would not be severe, and the amount could not readily be determined, the following qualified opinion would be given:

> In our opinion, except for the effects of adjustments that might have been required, if any, for the matters described in the preceding paragraphs, the financial statements referred to above present fairly the financial position of X company at December 31, 1984, and the results of its operations and changes in financial position for the year then ended.

Comments

In the adverse opinion and the disclaimer of opinion, the auditor says, in effect, "Be careful. We think there is a serious problem."

[2]Italics not in original.

In the qualified opinion, the auditor discloses the facts, and lets you make your own conclusion.

"Present Fairly"

You will note that the key words in the above opinions are *present fairly*. These words had not been defined until July 1975 when the AICPA Auditing Standards Executive Committee issued Statement on Auditing Standards (SAS)—No. 5, which says, in part:

> The independent auditor's judgment concerning the "fairness" of the overall presentation of financial statements should be applied within the framework of generally accepted accounting principles. Without that framework the auditor would have no uniform standard for judging the presentation of financial position, results of operations, and changes in financial position in financial statements.
>
> The auditor's opinion that financial statements present fairly an entity's financial position, results of operations, and changes in financial position in conformity with generally accepted accounting principles should be based on his judgment as to whether (a) the accounting principles selected and applied have general acceptance; (b) the accounting principles are appropriate in the circumstances; (c) the financial statements, including the related notes, are informative of matters that may affect their use, understanding, and interpretation***; (d) the information presented in the financial statements is classified and summarized in a reasonable manner, that is, neither too detailed nor too condensed*** and (e) the financial statements reflect the underlying events and transactions in a manner that presents the financial position, results of operations, and changes in financial position stated within a range of acceptable limits, that is, limits that are reasonable and practicable to attain in financial statements.[3]

An Example: The Manville Story

The Manville Corporation has become involved in major litigation consisting of thousands of cases concerning asbestos-related health injuries alleged to have resulted from exposure over the years to former employees, employees of the United States Government working on installing asbestos products in warships and other government-owned facilities, and employees of other corporations. These cases started to mushroom with an increasing contingent liability that now appears to be significant.

In its Form 10-Q filed under the SEC, the company reported, as follows:

[3]The concept of materiality is inherent in the auditors' judgments. That concept involves qualitative as well as quantitative judgments.

	Average number of new cases per month	Average number of new plaintiffs per month
1979	140	210
1980	230	365
1981—approximately	400	560
1982 prior to filing under Chapter 11— approximately	425	500
1982 subsequent to the commencement of Chapter 11 proceedings	350	725
1983 through June 30, 1983	63	64

The company believes that any lawsuits filed subsequent to the commencement of the Chapter 11 proceedings were filed in violation of the Bankruptcy Court's restraining order and the automatic stay provisions of the Bankruptcy Code.

On August 26, 1982, the company and twenty of its subsidiaries filed for bankruptcy under Chapter 11 of the Bankruptcy Act even though the company is not insolvent.

Dividends on the preferred and common stock have ceased and the market prices of the securities have plummetted (see table at end of this chapter) but during 1983 have recovered part of the loss. As of October 31, 1983 the common stock sold at $12.125. There were early warning signals long before the drop in market prices.

An alert stockholder would have been aware of what was happening because of the great amount of publicity given to this in the newspapers and financial periodicals. However, the first real signal was in the accountants' report issued by Coopers & Lybrand in connection with the December 31, 1980, consolidated financial statements and its comparison with the 1979 report. The following is the middle paragraph of the accountants' report:[4]

As discussed in Note 5 to the consolidated financial statements, the Company is a defendant in a substantial and increased number of asbestos/health legal actions. The ultimate liability resulting from these matters cannot presently be reasonably estimated. In our report dated February 1, 1980, *our opinion on the Company's consolidated financial position as of December 31, 1979 was unqualified. However, because of the increased uncertainties* that developed during 1980 with respect to these

[4]For those readers who want to read the full accountant's report and the full note to the consolidated financial statements, reference is made to the Appendix Nos. 2-3-4. The italics in all the quotations are mine.

matters, *our present opinion* on the consolidated financial position as of December 31, 1979, as presented herein, is different from that expressed in our previous report.

The following is the final opinion paragraph of this accountants' report and is very significant:

In our opinion, based upon our examinations and the report of other auditors, the aforementioned financial statements present fairly the consolidated results of operations and changes in financial position of Johns-Manville Corporation for each of the three years in the period ended December 31, 1980 *and, subject to the effects of adjustments that might have been required had the outcome of the uncertainties referred to in the preceding paragraph been known*, the consolidated financial position of Johns-Manville Corporation at December 31, 1980 and 1979, in conformity with generally accepted accounting principles applied on a consistent basis.

The language in the accountants' report becomes stronger with respect to the years ended December 31, 1981, and retroactively to 1980. The middle paragraph has been shortened to the following:

As discussed in Note 5 to the consolidated financial statements, Johns-Manville Corporation (a wholly-owned subsidiary of Manville Corporation) is a defendant in a substantial number of asbestos-health legal actions. The *ultimate liability* resulting from these matters *cannot presently be reasonably estimated*.

The following is the accountants' opinion for 1981 and revised for 1980:

In our opinion, based upon our examinations and the report of other auditors, the aforementioned financial statements present fairly the consolidated results of operations and changes in financial position of Manville Corporation for each of the three years in the period ended December 31, 1981 and, *subject to the effects of adjustments that might have been required had the outcome of the uncertainties referred to in the preceding paragraph been known*, the consolidated financial position of Manville Corporation at December 31, 1981 and 1980 in conformity with generally accepted accounting principles applied on a consistent basis.

The accountants' report in the 1982 annual report is the same as for the prior year. Reference is made in the middle paragraph of the report to the discussion in "Note 1—Chapter 11 Proceedings," which is reproduced in its entirety in Appendix 4. Reference is made therein to "Item 3, Legal Proceedings."

The 1982 annual report to stockholders incorporates data required in Manville's Annual Report on Form 10K to the SEC. "Item 3—Legal Proceedings" is part of the annual report on Form 10K and consists of

12½ pages of legal discussion. If you are interested in the details of the litigations and have not received a copy of this report, it can be obtained from the company.

The real impact upon the market prices of the common stock is principally in the fourth quarter of 1981 and during 1982. It is quite evident that a knowledgeable reader of the annual report who knew what to look for in the auditors' opinion could have formed a judgment as to the increasing risk and would have been alerted to follow the news very closely. Based upon all the factors involved in his investment, the stock could have been sold at any time during this period thereby avoiding a substantial loss, as can be noted from the following tabulation of high and low common-stock prices from 1979 through 1982.

	During year	
	High	Low
1979 During quarter ended		
September 30	27¾	
December 31		21⅞
1980 During quarter ended		
September 30	31⅜	
March 31		18¼
1981 During quarter ended		
March 31	26½	
December 31		13¾
1982 During quarter ended		
March 31	16½	
December 31		4¼
1983 (To Sept 30) during quarter ended		
June 30	16⅝	
March 31		10

SUMMARY

Most of the material in this chapter is technical but important. As long as you understand the significance of the standard auditors' opinion and are alerted to look further in connection with any deviation, you have learned a valuable lesson.

5

The Proxy Statement

This chapter is about the invitation to the annual stockholders' meeting, the official notice of the meeting, and the proxy statement. The first part of the chapter will give some background material and technical information that may be of interest to some readers but will not contribute much to the reader's ability to siphon that material and data that will enable him to make sound investment decisions. Of course, if it is of interest, read it, but if you want to, you can skip the first half and go directly to the paragraph captioned "Notice of Annual Meeting to Stockholders," where I begin the discussion of the information disclosed which will add to your knowledge toward making sound investment decisions.

DEFINITION OF PROXY

Because the authority for the regulations of proxies arises out of Section 14 of the Securities and Exchange Act of 1934, I thought I could find there a good definition for the word *proxy*. This section of the Act refers to ". . . such rules and regulations as the Commission may prescribe as necessary or appropriate in the public interest or for the protection of investors to solicit or permit the use of his name to solicit any proxy or consent or authorization in respect of any security registered under Section 12 of this title."

That wasn't very helpful, so I thought that I would next look into the Regulations. Rule 14A-1 of Regulation 14A, "Solicitation of Proxies," defines *proxy* as follows: "The term 'proxy' includes every proxy or consent or authorization within the meaning of Section 14A of the Act. The consent or authorization may take the form of failure to object or to dissent."

That didn't help much either, so I went to the best source I know for definitions—*Webster's New World Dictionary of the American Language, Second College Edition.* It says that a proxy is:

- The authority to act for another
- A document empowering a person to act for another, as in voting for a stockholders' meeting
- A person empowered to act for another.

Now I know, and I hope you know too.

THE INVITATION

Although it is not required by the regulations, many companies write a letter to their shareholders inviting them to attend the annual meeting or, if they cannot attend, to submit their proxies. This accompanies the notice of Annual Meeting of Shareholders and the Proxy Statement.

The regulations provide that ". . . if the solicitation is made on behalf of the issuer and relates to an annual meeting of security holders at which directors are to be elected, each proxy statement furnished pursuant to paragraph (a), *shall be accompanied or preceded by an annual report to such security holders as follows*"[1] and then describes what the report is to include. To show the extent to which the regulations spell out how this solicitation of proxies should be handled, it even goes so far as to describe that all printed proxy statements shall be in Roman type at least as large and as legible as ten-point Modern type.

The following briefly discusses the rules and regulations:

[1]Italics mine.

STRUCTURE OF THE REGULATIONS

The definition quoted above from the Act gives the SEC the authority and duty to issue regulations and rules. These regulations, like most government regulations are rather complex, consist of fourteen rules.

At the next layer of information we have Schedules, of which the most important is Schedule 14A, entitled, "Information Required by Proxy Statement," consisting of twenty-two items. For our purposes, the schedules become more important and we will discuss these later.

Item 15, "Financial Statements and Supplementary Data," is the most important item and says in part, "If action is to be taken with respect to any matter [items] specified . . . above, furnish the financial statements requested by Regulation S-X and the supplementary financial information requested by Item 12 of Regulations S-K."

Regulation S-X has the formidable title of "Form and Content of and Requirements for Financial Statements, Securities Act of 1933, Securities Exchange Act of 1934, Public Utility Holding Company Act of 1935, Investment Company Act of 1940 and Energy Policy and Conservation Act of 1975." Among other things, this regulation requires the following:

- Qualifications and reports of accountants
- General instructions as to the financial statements, including the prescribed forms and contents of schedules required by several of the rules.
- Consolidated and combined financial statements
- Rules of general application
- Special rules for different types of industries
- Form and content of schedules

Regulation S-X has become the bible for financial officers, company accountants of public companies, and their independent auditors and certified public accountants.

On December 30, 1977, the SEC adopted Integrated Disclosure Regulation S-K, which amended Regulation S-X and certain disclosure forms and rules so as to integrate the information presented in registration statements, annual reports, proxy statements, and information statements. Some became effective for fiscal years beginning after December 15, 1976, and others effective for fiscal years ended after March 15, 1978. In effect, Regulation S-K added industry segment reporting and required many other changes that should help investors to analyze and understand reported information and data.

There are no special requirements as to the sequence of these items in the proxy statement, and I will follow the sequence most commonly used.

Proxy statements vary greatly. It can be only a few pages long or, if the meeting is going to be very active, can consist of many pages including copies of important documents as required. We will relate basically to the common proxy statement for an annual shareholders' meeting.

A brief opening statement will usually contain the following information:

1. Date mailed
2. Persons making the solicitation
3. Date, time, and location of the meeting
4. That if the proxy is duly executed and returned, it will be voted in accordance with the specification made by the shareholder
5. Revocability of the proxy
6. The record date of shareholders having the right to receive the notice and to vote at the annual meeting
7. The number of shares then outstanding
8. A brief statement of the shareholder's rights
9. Other matters that are deemed desirable for a brief statement by the corporation.

Most of this material is not particularly significant and can be quickly scanned.

Notice of Annual Meetings to Stockholders

The notice of annual meeting to shareholders is the official document advising the stockholder of the date, time, and location of the annual meeting. It includes that important document, the proxy statement, which is the information described in Scheduld 14A. All of the items required are discussed hereinafter, not necessarily in the sequence in which they are included in the regulations. Some of the twenty-two items are not of sufficient importance to be included in each proxy statement. I will discuss only those of importance and indicate the item number for identification purposes so that, if you so desire, you may go to the regulations and read the specific requirements.

The Notice of Annual Meeting need not be read except for a quick look at the tabulation of the matters to be acted upon to see if there is anything unusual or interesting that you might want to read about in the proxy statement.

The Proxy

Six samples of proxy forms are suggested in the rules. They usually are IBM cards that can be processed by a computer.

It is suggested in most instances that you indicate your choices, sign the proxy, and mail it in.

It is also suggested that you attend those meetings that are held within your geographical area, if you have time. A meeting usually takes a part of a day, mostly the mornings. Attend a few of them; if time permits, attend more than a few. They are educational and interesting and will give you good insight into the management of the company, of other stockholders, and the interest that exists in the operation of your company.

Directors and Executive Officers (Item 6)

Item 6 is the basic description of information required about the election of directors. It is amended by Item 3 of Regulation S-K, which spells out in detail what information is required in the proxy statement. This generally is a list of the directors, specifying which are to be voted upon at the meeting, and requires furnishing a biographical summary of each nominee, including the period of time that each was a director and the business affiliation of each. Some of the larger companies include a picture of each nominee. Other companies merely furnish the minimum information to satisfy the regulations.

It is important to look at this information to evaluate the competence, experience, and ability of the directors, their role in the company, and their relationship to management. The board of directors generally consists of several top management executives of the corporation, such as chairman of the board, president, certain vice presidents, and so on. The others are all considered independent.

From the viewpoint of an investor, the following should be considered:

- **Independence:** the extent to which members of the board are not associated in any way with those involved with day-to-day management. It is assumed that such directors can give objective consideration to the matters brought before the board.
- **Stature of outsiders:** This is indicative of what they can contribute to establishing broad management policies.
- **Period of service:** It takes time to get thoroughly familiar with a large corporation. The period of service of each board member might be useful in determining the quality and stability of the board.

- **Number of meetings held and attendance of each member:** An effective board should consist of members who attend the majority of the meetings. This will also help you to evaluate how serious the members take their responsibilities and their stewardship for the stockholders.
- **Age of each of the members:** The members of a well-constituted board should vary in age so that retirements are staggered. Furthermore, staggered ages give a better cross section of business acumen and experience in the board as a whole.
- **Compensation:** Outside board members should be properly compensated for the time and effort that is required for them to appropriately meet the responsibilities of their stewardship.
- **Changes in the composition of the board:** A quick comparison of the membership of the current board of directors with the previous year's board would disclose whether there had been changes and how many. If there are a number of changes, it may suggest that there are some problems brewing and should alert the stockholder to potential trouble.

A board of directors is usually organized into committees that meet separately from the board. The committees most commonly noted and the complexion of the committee as to outsiders and insiders are listed below:

Executive Committee: mixed

Audit Committee: outsiders

Nominating Committee: mixed

Remuneration Committee: mixed

Officers Options and Bonuses Committee: usually outsiders

Most committees are small, consisting of perhaps two, three, four, or five members, depending upon the committee's responsibilities and the size of the total board. The number of meetings held and the attendance of the members is an important and interesting fact that should be observed.

Remuneration of Directors and Executive Officers (Item 7)

A tabulation of the top officers of the company is presented showing their names, the capacity in which each serves, and salaries and other fees and remuneration, securities, property, insurance benefits and other fringe items, income from incentive plans and deferred awards, and so on. This is shown for each of the top officers, plus there is a total for all the directors and officers as a group, indicating the numbers of persons included. The amounts represent some staggering numbers for big corporations, but when the amounts are equated with the revenues and income of these corporations, it is understood why these people are entitled to such large sums. This is an area that is more significant in the smaller public companies, where it might appear that the board of directors is controlled by top management or where a small group of stockholders control the corporation and are running the business for their own benefit, leaving only small amounts available for dividends to stockholders.

Fringe benefits are usually described in detail, covering such matters as incentive plans, stock bonus plans, employment contracts, retirement benefits, and pensions. Such items need not be read but just scanned in most instances.

Pension and Retirement Plans and Options, Warrants, or Rights (Items 10 and 11)

The proxy statement requires the reporting of the retirement program and stock option plans describing the benefits to those officers listed under remuneration for directors and officers. This should be scanned for reasonableness.

Voting Securities and Principal Holders Thereof (Item 5)

It is required to tabulate the voting shares owned, beneficially by the officers and directors or where persons listed have voting power. Disclosure is made of spouses' holdings or trusts in which the individuals have some authority or benefits.

This list should be scanned to see how much control of voting shares rests with insiders. Outsiders who are not members of the board must also be reported if they are beneficial owners in excess of 5 percent.

The above recitation of those sections of the proxy statement pertaining to the top management and the board of directors is significant to evaluate the management of the company.

- The management must be stable. In other words, the turnover should be slow, but steady.
- The management should be knowledgeable and competent and have experience in lines of business or activities that can contribute in a great way to the progress and well-being of the corporation.
- Good management is one of the keys to a successful operation.
- Poor management can dissipate assets and impair the progress of a company fairly rapidly.

For these reasons, it is suggested that this be one of the first areas examined when reviewing the proxy statement and the annual report.

Relationship with Independent Public Accountants (Item 8)

The stockholders vote to confirm, ratify, approve, or appoint the independent auditors or certified public accountants for the corporation for the following fiscal year. Certain information is required to be reported; this can be scanned quickly and examined to see whether there are any unusual comments made. This is usually a routine matter that continues the existing relationship.

Proposals by Security Holders (Rule 14a-8)

Proposals can be made by shareholders on various subjects for presentation to all of the shareholders at the annual meeting. This is usually done in the form of a resolution with a statement by the proposer as to why they want the stockholders to vote "yes." In most instances, the corporation makes a statement of its opposition and that the board of directors recommends a vote against the shareholder's proposal.

There may be proposals by certain independent groups and independent shareholders whose names appear frequently in proxy statements, such as Lewis D. and John J. Gilbert; Evelyn Davis; Wilma Soss (they are sometimes referred to as gadflies)—for the Federation of Women Shareholders in American Business, Inc.; Institute for Public Representation; various religious groups; various labor unions. These proposals generally may be scanned so that you can decide how you want to vote on the matters involved. These proposals usually are rejected except in the rare occasion when management approves.

Rule 14a-8 establishes the procedures, disclosures, and requirements to include the proposal of these groups and shareholders in the proxy statement.

Other Items

There are a number of items in Schedule 14a that do not appear regularly in proxy statements and vary from relatively unimportant to quite significant. Some are listed below.

Item 2: Dissenters' Right of Appraisal. There may be resolutions in the proxy statement that must be acted upon and upon which a shareholder dissents, feeling that he will be injured if they are passed. If such occasions arise, the stockholder has a legal right of appraisal of the loss that could be sustained. A statement to this effect may be required in the proxy statement. If it is included, do not bother reading it unless you think it pertains to you. If it does scan it or read it thoroughly.

Item 12: Authorization of or Issuance of Securities Otherwise than for Exchange

Item 13: Modification or Change of Securities

Item 14: Mergers, Consolidations, Acquisitions and Similar Matters

Item 16: Acquisition or Disposition of Property

Item 17: Restatement of Accounts

Item 18: Action with Respect to Reports. This represents reports made to the stockholders of matters that might be of interest and where the stockholders' approval of the action taken is requested.

Item 19: Matters Not Required to be Submitted. The board of directors or the management might want to submit to the shareholders a matter or several matters for approval or ratification that are not necessarily required to be approved or ratified by the shareholders as a whole.

Item 20: Amendment of Charter, By-Laws or Other Documents

Item 21: Other Proposed Action. This is a catch-all item to cover anything not covered elsewhere.

Of the items listed, some instances may require a merger plan, restatement of accounts, authorization, issuance, modification, or exchange of securities, accompanied by a summary by management of what is intended and why the stockholder should vote for it. Copies of the official documents are often part of the proxy statement.

It is suggested that the management summary be scanned or read in detail so that judgment can be given as to how you will vote on these matters. Frequently the pros and cons are mentioned in the comments by management explaining why you should give your approval for their proposal. If you have confidence in the management, it is simple to make a judgment decision. The less confidence you have in the integrity of the board of directors and internal management, the more you should study the problems. On occasion these matters may also be reported on by a dissenting group of stockholders who publicize their opposing views. Sometimes you may receive proxy statements from both groups. In that event, you have a problem on your hands and you should study each proxy statement carefully.

Vote Required for Approval

As to each matter that is submitted to a vote by security holders, other than election of members of the board or the selection or approval of auditors, the proxy statement states the percentage vote required for approval. This is generally no serious matter requiring judgment.

SUMMARY

This has been a fairly long discussion of the proxy statement. It is an innocuous- and dull-looking document with a lot of legalese and is rarely studied by the average stockholder, who would rather look at the annual report with its color and pretty pictures prepared by the public relations department. It would appear that the time applied to reading the proxy statement could be most fruitful.

At the beginning, it might be a chore to study the proxy statement in this manner. However, after you have looked at a number of them, you can become fairly knowledgeable of the usual contents and what to look for. You will quickly learn what is meaningful and what will have a bearing upon the value of your investment. As we said earlier, know your company, know the company's industry, and know its management. By knowing your company, you can quickly evaluate whether things are the way they should be and how much or how little time you should devote to reading the various matters disclosed in the proxy statement.

6

The Contents
of an Annual Report

The Stockholder's Annual Report—or, as it is sometimes called, Annual Report to Shareholders, and most frequently just the Annual Report—is the principal direct communication from management to its shareholders and is an annual opportunity management has to discuss the operations of the company in detail. Most companies make full use of this opportunity. In addition, many of the companies submit quarterly reports that are very brief versions of the financial statements with a short communication to the stockholders about current activities.

PURPOSE OF THIS CHAPTER

There are several things that influence the contents of the annual report. The SEC probably has the greatest influence upon the contents. The Financial Accounting Standards Board (FASB) principally and the American Institute of Certified Public Accountants (AICPA) have a significant influence upon the financial statements and the related notes thereto as well as the auditor's opinion.

Although it is not necessary, many companies use the talents in their advertising and marketing staffs or retain advertising and promotion agencies to help make the report as attractive as possible for the shareholders, the financial analysts, or any readers who may be interested in the company. The cost of this whole package is substantial, with all these people involved, not to mention the time put in by the appropriate members of the company's management team.

Of course, annual reports vary from a very simple black-and-white eight-page booklet to a booklet of many pages with color pictures, charts, diagrams, financial schedules, tables, and general information about the company that, in some instances, becomes quite a volume. The reports all make interesting reading.

The purpose of this chapter is to list and describe the various sections in the average annual report of a good-sized company listed on the New York Stock Exchange, the American Stock Exchange, and those traded on the over-the-counter markets.

THE COVERS

The covers are used to furnish you with certain pertinent information. The front page usually carries a very attractive picture and is directed toward the theme of this year's annual report or to some major aspect of the company's operation.

The inside of the first page of the cover usually has information such as:

Date and place of annual meeting
Names of Transfer agents and Registrar of stock
Principal addresses of the company
The fact that a copy of Form 10-K is available upon request at the company's basic address
Perhaps a brief description of the company
The table of contents.

On the back cover, the report might have a list of the principal locations, branches, subsidiaries, or divisions of the company and a list of the members of the board of directors and officers. The outside of the back cover is frequently left blank or may provide for the mailing address of the stockholder.

TABLE OF CONTENTS

The following describes the average table of contents:

Messages to Stockholders: This may be called the president's letter or the chairman's letter, or both.

Financial Summary: Sometimes called "Financial Data in Summary Form"; it includes information for the current year and the two prior years.

The Company's Report to Stockholders: This is a section of text, pictures, charts, and statistics by which a company discusses any subject about its operations, competitors, the economy, the past, the future, and so on, all based upon this year's theme. Almost any title that describes the theme is appropriate.

Discussion of Products and Services Sold: In between the messages to stockholders and the financial review there usually is a series of sections about the products, services, and operations of the company. This is some of the best work prepared by the marketing divisions and the business promotion departments with all the glamour that is developed by them for glossy advertising. Throughout the rhetoric, which is really a sales pitch, there might be some information that you as a shareholder will find interesting, valuable, and useful. Only you can judge how much time and effort you want to devote to the reading of this material.

Review of Operations: This is required by the SEC and will be mentioned in a later chapter.

Financial Review: This section also is required by the SEC and is a discussion by management comparing the past three years' operations with one another.

Financial Statements: This is the guts of the annual report. It includes the financial statements that are explained in detail in Chapter 9.

Auditors' Opinion: This is the only portion of the report that is the total responsibility of the auditors. However, in order to give this opinion, the auditors' work has a tremendous impact on all of the financial data and even some of the textual material in the annual report.

Management's Responsibility: Sometimes called Management's Report, it explains the extent of the auditors' responsibility as compared with management's responsibility for the financial statements of the company. It explains how the company establishes policies and procedures to fulfill its obligation to its stockholders to fairly report the financial position and results.

Major Markets: This section is different for different companies. Some of them will list the various markets to whom they sell their products; others will list the major divisions and subsidiaries.

The following comments about each section discusses the significance and the amount of vital information that you may obtain.

Messages to Stockholders

The message may be by the chairman of the board with another letter by the president, but sometimes the two sign a single message. It is an opportunity for these two top officials of the company to express their views about what happened in the past year and perhaps what may happen in the future.

If the company is doing well, this is the opportunity for them to say how well they have managed the company and brag a bit about their accomplishments. If it has been a poor year and the earnings are flat or down, an effort is made, at times, to whitewash the mediocre operations. The blame could be given to the economic conditions, the high cost of labor, the inability to increase selling prices, the high cost of raw materials, the political climate, the present administration, and/ or a host of other matters. Another explanation in recent years has been the high cost of money and high interest rates and their impact upon the economy, causing a recession.

If a company is not doing well, the president's letter might refer to a restructuring of the company or redeployment of assets, the disposal of nonprofitable units. In that event, the financial statements reflect the results of continuing operations, which usually look good, and separates the discontinuing operations that caused the poor showing and loss.

At times reference is made to the chairman of the board as chief executive officer and the president as chief operating officer. It is very difficult in each situation to understand just what each means, because responsibilities are not clear and, in most instances, may be joint. The chairman of the board is usually senior, having been president for some years, and the younger individual having succeeded the chairman as president and chief operating officer.

There are usually a few vital comments in these letters and also some promotional remarks. As a general rule, it might be desirable just to skim through the letters and if you see some numbers, read that section. Perhaps by glancing through it some other phrases might catch your eye that would indicate a section of real significance for you to read.

Don't pass this section by completely—there is always something to be learned. It also may give you some valuable insight into the management.

Financial Summary

The "Financial Summary" section will give you an overall view of the financial operations for two or three years with the percentage of increases or decreases. It shows key numbers with more details available later in the financial statements. You can tell quickly from this summary whether the volume of sales has increased, whether earnings have increased, and also the earnings and dividends per share. Some companies also show the stock price range during the past fiscal year.

This section is worth close scrutiny.

The Company's Report to Stockholders

"The Company's Report to Stockholders" can be almost anything. In some reports this is the president's letter; in others it is the text that talks about the company's operations, products, new plants, each of the segments of the business, or any subject the company may want to discuss. Many include factual material that requires more than casual examination. This section often gives an analysis of the operations by industry segments with operating charts of performance of each. It is meaningful data.

This is the portion of the report with all the promotion department's art, pretty pictures, advertising blurbs, colorful charts, and attractive presentations.

As you review the stockholder's report for your company, you can determine whether it is necessary to read this section thoroughly, give it a modest review, or just scan it.

Financial Review and Financial Statements

The "Financial Review and Financial Statements" section has several parts that are very important. I have combined these two items because the individual parts follow no usual sequence, are often commingled, and all relate to one another. They include the following:

- The management discussion and comparison of three years' financial data
- Consolidated Statement of Earnings, sometimes called Consolidated Statement of Income
- Consolidated Statement of Retained Earnings
- Consolidated Balance Sheets
- Consolidated Statement of Changes in Financial Position
- Notes to Consolidated Financial Statements
- Auditors' Opinion, sometimes called Accountant's Report
- Management's Responsibility, sometimes called Management Report on Financial Statements
- Ten-Year Financial and Operating Summary

If the corporate structure of the company is a single corporation, the word *consolidated* is not included. Most investment entities consist of a parent company and one or more subsidiaries, hence the inclusion of *consolidated* in the title. The consolidated financial statements are prepared to reflect the operations as if the group were one company. In all instances throughout this book, the word *company* means both a single corporation or a consolidated group.

All of the Consolidated Statements and the Notes to the Financial Statements are covered by the umbrella of the Auditors' Opinion. Depending upon your interest in amounts and your ability to understand these complex statements you may want to spend a lot of time reading them. For the average reader, I suggest that you refer to Chapter 9, which is a discussion, in detail, of each of these statements and the importance of each.

The most significant statement for you is the Ten-Year Summary, which can give you a good understanding of how the company has been doing throughout the years and what progress it is making. The Ten-Year Summaries vary somewhat in content, but all have the most important information and statistical data that is significant. This is also discussed further in Chapter 9.

Management Markets: Divisions and Subsidiaries

The "Divisions and Subsidiaries" section is not infrequently on the last pages or on the inside of the back cover. It is of interest to you to evaluate the kind of business you are investing in. It would answer some of the following questions: Is it the kind of company that you want to invest your money in? Is its business in markets that interest you? Is it the kind of company that you think will have a future, that will pay you the dividends you want in the future? Will the products and services it sells improve the market value of your stock at a rate faster than inflation?

There are no specifics I can give you other than to urge you to use your good judgment based upon your experience and upon what you read in the newspapers and in the magazines and follow the contents of this and other books on investments.

Miscellaneous Items to Look for

There are a number of miscellaneous things that may appear from time to time in an annual report.

There are some companies that mention changes in management. If you had confidence in the previous management, you may consider whether these changes have the potential to alter your opinion. On the other hand, if the company hasn't been doing well and there is a significant change in management, it might indicate a change for the better. On the other hand, it might suggest existing and future problems. Discuss the change with your broker, who might have insight into this sort of situation.

The only place to look for a prognostication of what the future has in store is in the messages from the chairman of the board and the president. There may be a lengthy or just a limited discussion about the future depending upon the attitude of the company's management and their willingness to stick their neck out by telling what the next few years may have in store.

You may find some comments about a change from the previous year resulting from mergers, restructuring, or divestitures. In some companies a special section is included in the annual report to cover such items. I cannot give any specific suggestions about such changes. Just study the changes and use your best judgment. Communicate with the company. Perhaps you can get some answers from its officers.

If there are major changes in the product lines or very important new products, this is frequently reported in a separate section in the annual report. This is well worth reading.

Another very significant item is the statistical data that is available for certain industries. For example, oil producers may indicate the number of successful wells and the number of barrels produced during the year in comparison with other years. Railroads could indicate operating miles; airlines, passengers' miles flown; housing, the number of housing starts; hotel operations, number of rooms available or rented or vacancy percentages, and so on.

It goes back to the old story: Know your company. Volume statistics often give a better picture of what is going on than dollar statistics.

SUMMARY

What has been said herein gives you some guidelines for reading annual reports. Each report is the unique product of the company and its management. Some managements are as secretive as they can be within the requirements of the SEC and the FASB. Other companies' managements try to bare their soul to the fullest extent up to the point that it would not impair their status against their competition.

The trend has been to give more information each year rather than less. This trend has been fostered by the SEC, the accounting profession, and the Financial Accounting Standards Board. One of the greater influences is that of the more progressive companies who are leaders in their industry. Others try to follow in their footsteps.

As a final word of caution, annual reports are not always the most current information about a company. The earliest that these can be published by the best-managed companies is during the early part of the second month following the end of the fiscal year. Many companies take two to three months to issue the reports and get it into the hands of the stockholders. Keep apace of current events by constant reading of the appropriate daily newspapers. Read as many selected business magazines as you have time for and try to be in constant communication with your stockbroker. If your account is big enough and your broker is good and alert, he or she will let you know if any important matter about your company comes over the ticker tape. That is about the most current bit of public information that you can get.

7

The Numbers Game

If you have a facility with numbers, for example, if you got an A in algebra or have been a bookkeeper or worked in an accounting department or are an engineer, you won't need the information contained in this chapter. However, if you are like many people (some of whom are rather astute investors) and are mystified by numbers, you might gain some confidence and knowledge by reading what follows.

A number—for example, 6,859,743—standing alone by itself is not very meaningful. Even if there is a name before the number, such as "Net income," you cannot place any judgment upon it. This number must be compared with another number to add some value to it, such as "Net income $5,343,609." Now you know that the first number is larger than the second one. If one represented net income for 1982 and the other for 1981, you can readily determine that there has been an increase in earnings. But you still haven't got a basis for determining the significance.

Numbers must be identified and, in order to make them useful, must be compared with something, either a number that you already have in mind or with other numbers that you are reading about. This is precisely what a person does when he or she goes shopping. That person is constantly making comparisons. Either the price is higher or lower than yesterday's or it is a bargain compared with the price of the other item with a different label; or maybe it is too costly because it doesn't fit one's budget. This is the kind of comparison that is easily done, and it is somewhat similar to the comparisons made analyzing the stockholders' annual report.

Most people have difficulty evaluating the large numbers, the millions of dollars and, in some cases, billions of dollars because, in their day-to-day living, they don't deal with such large numbers. They can't compare them with anything they normally understand. However, recognizing this, most annual reports include numbers that are meaningful and can be compared with an amount that the investor can recognize, understand, and relate to everyday living.

For example, I have taken some data directly from the "Results in Brief" statement of the 1980 Annual Report of the American Telephone & Telegraph Company. This says that net income for 1980 is $6,080 million, which you can readily convert to $6 billion. Standing alone, this is a big number, but what does it mean to the investor? In the same statement it refers to $5,674 million net income for 1979, which is roughly $5.7 billion. Now there is a little bit more information that is available. We do notice that there has been an increase in net income of about $400 million between 1979 and 1980. It's beginning to make a little more sense, but it still is hard to evaluate. In another line in the same section, AT&T reports earnings per common share of $8.19, compared with $8.04 in 1979. Here are numbers that the average person can comprehend. You know immediately what you can buy for $8.19 and also have some other information already in mind. You now know that for each share you own, the company has earned $8.19, which is $0.15 more than last year. If you have been keeping up with the news, you know that the current price per share of AT&T is $55. There now is a clear-cut comparison that means something. By dividing $55 by $8.19, you arrive at 6.7. This is the price/earnings ratio. Stated another way, the market value of the stock is almost seven times one year's earnings for that share of stock. It is not necessary to make this computation because the price/earnings ratios for all common stocks are quoted in the daily newspaper in the column with "P-E Ratio" heading.

In the same statement the company reports that the dividend declared per common share is $5. Again this is something that is readily understood. You as the stockholder know that for the 100 shares of stock that you own you will receive $125 each quarter, which will equal $500 for the year. You also can relate the amount of the earnings that accrued to your benefit of $8.19 per share, $3.19 is retained by the company for future growth and as a cushion to guarantee that the $5 paid annually is a dividend that reasonably can be expected to continue or perhaps increase.

If the investor wants to compare the net income of American Telephone and Telegraph with that of General Telephone and Electronics Company, (now GTE Corp.) the comparison of $6,080 million net income compared with the $587 million of GTE reported in the annual report for 1980 merely is just an indication of the relative size of the company, which does not necessarily give information as to the per share earning ability. However, when the $3.87 per share amount is read in the GTE Financial Highlights Statement, you have a number that can be compared quite readily with $8.19 of AT&T. In other words, you can readily see that per share of stock, At&T earns slightly more than twice that earned by GTE. But, again, we have to look at some other numbers for further comparisons. Relating to the market price of GTE of $30 per share, a clearer picture shows up. The highlight shows that the dividends of GTE for the year 1980 was $2.72, or $272 per 100 shares of stock. A simple comparison can now be made between the two companies for investment purposes. Assume that dividends earned is an important characteristic of your investment program. One hundred shares of AT&T cost $5,500 and would result in dividend income of $500 a year. The investment of $6,000 in GTE would result in the purchase of 200 shares, which would pay an annual dividend of $544. Just by looking at these simple numbers one can readily see that there is not much difference between the two companies with respect to earnings on investments. However, if this were the only guide it would appear that AT&T is the better investment because you would earn 9 percent on your $6,000 investment in GTE as compared with 9.1 percent on your $5,500 investment in AT&T.

This is merely a small exercise in how you can find the small numbers in the annual report that you can relate to your everyday life.

If you use this type of information presented in the highlights of an annual report, you can make investing decisions that require practically no pencil pushing on your part. However, it might be simplified by making a small tabulation similar to the following, putting side by side certain statistics that can be readily found in the annual report.

Recognizing that the significance of small numbers can be more readily understood by common stockholders, companies, in discussing the results of operations, frequently state them in terms of per share value so that a stockholder can relate how much is attributable to his holdings. Furthermore, the average stockholder can ignore all the major numbers in the annual report and only read the per share numbers or the percentage data that is included in the consolidated highlights and in the Ten-Year Financial Summaries, which quickly give a picture of the past results and what can be expected in the future.

	AT&T	GTE
Gross revenues	$51,680 (M)	$9.979 (M)
Net income	6,080 (M)	587 (A)(M)
Earnings per common share	8.19	3.87
Dividends declared	5.00	2.72
Market prices	55	30
Equivalent shares	100	200
Cost	5,500	6,000
Dividend income	500	544
Percent earned	9.1%	9%
Price earnings ratio	6.7%	7.7%

(A) From continuing operations
(M) Million dollars

The financial highlights of five years can quickly disclose to you how the net worth of the company has grown, if it has grown. It also can show how earnings have changed throughout the years. A steady earnings rate is usually pretty good, provided the increase in net earnings per year per share of stock at least covers the inflation rate. Similarly, an increase in book value per share would also reflect good results, particularly if the annual increases exceed the rate of inflation. Such increases in per share earnings, dividends, and net worth usually result in increases in the market price per share of stock, providing there are no other matters that influence market prices.

Operating statements vary by industries. After looking at several annual reports for the same industry, you can readily get a feel of what is appropriate for the industry that interests you. By making comparisons between companies, a selection of the company that has demonstrated a steady and better growth than others in the industry might continue to do the same in the future, everything else being equal. This helps you make a decision.

To help in this regard, annual reports now include quarterly financial data and per share data for each quarter of the current year and the previous year and the high, low, and close market prices for each quarter of each year for common stock. Just scanning these charts could readily enable investors to understand how the operating results are reflected in the marketplace without doing any calculation on their part.

Some companies report earnings per share on two lines that might be confusing. The first is "Primary Earnings per Share" and the second is "Fully Diluted Earnings per Share." The computation of these two amounts is in accordance with rules established by the AICPA that are complex and technical. The following is a simplified discussion of the subject.

Many companies have convertible securities such as convertible bonds and convertible preferred stock that, at the option of the holder, can be converted, at certain ratios, into common stock. By definition, such a security, because of its terms or the circumstances under which it was issued, is in substance equivalent to common stock. Primary earnings per share are based on the actual outstanding common shares and common stock equivalents that do not have a dilutive effect, using the weighted average number of shares of common stock outstanding during the period.

The purpose of fully diluted earnings per share presentation is to show the maximum potential dilution of current earnings per share on a prospective basis.

In determining the fully diluted earnings per common share, the earnings per common share are determined and computed on the assumption that all the convertible securities and outstanding stock options and warrants were converted into common stock at the beginning of the year, thereby increasing the number of shares of common stock outstanding and also increasing the amount of earnings available for common stock by eliminating fixed dividends on the preferred stock or interest on the convertible bonds that need not be paid. The computation in arriving at fully diluted earnings per common share is to reflect the effect of options granted under contractual relations and employee option plans.

Since fully diluted earnings are always the lower of the two, and since the dilution is generally always a few cents, use the fully diluted for any decision determination. This is the conservative approach.

If you see an unusual tabulation of per share basis or of percentages that you do not understand, discuss it with the customer representative who handles your account at your broker's office. This is a knowledgeable person who has been dealing with such things constantly throughout the years and is familiar with the companies in which you own your shares and therefore can explain the significance and the importance of such data.

8

Management

Management is the most important asset of your company. When you invest, you entrust your hard-earned savings to these people and you should try to learn as much as you can about them. Unfortunately, the management that will make your company successful is like an iceberg; only the tip is showing. The tip is the board of directors and the corporate or executive officers.

THE BOARD OF DIRECTORS AND OFFICERS

Most major companies have a board consisting of about fifteen people and perhaps fifteen to twenty-five officers whose names appear in the annual report. In addition, other persons are operating management, and their names may appear in the annual report as officers of divisions, officers of subsidiaries, or managers of principal administrative functions, usually with the title of a division or group vice president or, in instances of subsidiaries, perhaps presidents. The names and backgrounds of the latter group are frequently not disclosed, and in no instance do the stockholders know about their backgrounds, experiences, and capabilities. They might be known within their own industry or profession, but not to the general public. Yet they manage important divisions and sections of your company. The success or failure of reaching the company's goal depends to a great extent on those people who are on the firing line, operating under the policies that are established by the board of directors implemented by the corporate or executive officers who issue the rules and guidelines for the operating officers.

A few of the corporate officers are usually on the board of directors, but in most cases they represent a minority of the board. In recent years it has been the objective of management to have outsiders constitute a majority of the board of directors to include members who are independent, objective individuals who are not involved in the day-to-day operation of the business. Yet it is evident that, with very few exceptions, these boards are self-perpetuating because it is very rare that the stockholders nominate members to the board. Nominees selected by the nominating committee of the board are almost always elected.

Usually the members of the board, other than insiders who are employee/officers, receive an annual stipend ranging from $10,000 to $25,000. In most companies the board of directors meets between ten and twelve times a year except if there are special circumstances that require special meetings. In addition, the outsiders serve on committees as discussed in Chapter 5.

The best information that you can get on the background, experience, and relationship to the company of the nominees is in the proxy statement mailed to you. The range of disclosure is broad. In some smaller companies it is only a short sentence or two, whereas the larger companies give complete one-paragraph biographical sketches of each of the members of the board, as well as photographs. They all indicate the number of shares of common stock beneficially owned and in many instances the percentage beneficially owned. This material is all discussed in detail in Chapter 5, which also describes how the board of directors is organized by committees.

As a stockholder, what can you expect from the board of directors and the corporate officers who have the stewardship of your investment with no opportunity for you to direct them in the use of these funds?

ELECTION OF OFFICERS

You must rely upon the board of directors to select and elect the corporate and executive officers. The board is guided in its search for approriate persons for each position by the nominating committee, if there is one. There are some companies which do not have a standing nominating committee but create one whenever there is a vacancy to be filled either on the board of directors or among the officers. Officer positions are often filled from the ranks of the younger operating officers, moving them up in an appropriate progression.

The operating officers of divisions and subsidiaries are generally appointed or elected by corporate officers or as a formality by the board of directors for each of the subsidiaries. You can readily see from this that the self-perpetuating management is really developed in what is often said with a smile a "very democratic process."

EVALUATING THE MANAGEMENT

How can you tell if the board of directors and the management officers are performing their duties in such a manner that you can depend upon their stewardship to do the best that they can for you? You can form a judgment from several things that are made available to you.

Of course, the first and clearest picture that you can get is from studying the biographies of each of the members of the board as detailed in the proxy statement. Determine to what extent the board is independent of the operating management. Is the board really a "watchdog" who can be critical and can challenge day-to-day management policies and decisions? Will the board members take action when the think the officers are acting improperly?

Since one of your objectives is to improve the value of your investment, a good guide as to whether management is doing its job appropriately is to examine the five-year or ten-year summary of earnings to see whether the earnings per share have been improving at an appropriate rate and thereby increasing the dividends, if any, that are being paid to you each year.

Another source of information is to determine whether management is effectively using cash flow for contributing toward the expansion and growth of your company. This can be observed by an examination of the Statement of Changes in Financial Position. Is a sufficient amount of the cash used to expand plant, renew plant, increase production facilities, or acquire companies? Is cash squirrelled away in such a manner for use to increase the salaries and incentive pay for the highly paid officers and the payment of limited dividends? Such a policy could be the case in a company in which a large percentage of the outstanding common stock is owned by one family or by a small group that controls the board and the management operating the company principally for the benefit of the insiders. Only the board of directors can declare dividends, and the independent members are there to protect your interests. Let's hope that they do.

LEVERAGE

Another thing to think about is whether the management is using "leverage" to enhance the position of the common stock stockholder. A general technique is to use borrowings or funded debt for the acquisition of facilities that will create cash flow to pay the interest, redeem the securities in a reasonable period of time, and at the same time contribute an increase to current and future earnings and perhaps increase dividends. The borrowing could be through bank loans or bonds sold to the public on Wall Street.

An effective source of leverage is through the issuance of convertible bonds. Such convertible bonds usually call for lower interest rates than bonds of the same quality that do not have the coversion feature. The conversion into common stock is usually accomplished after a significant increase in the market value of the common stock over and above the conversion price. This conversion would dilute the percentage equity of existing stockholders, but it is one of the best ways to obtain additional equity financing at minimum financing cost. While the bonds are still outstanding, the company has use of the money at a low-interest cost and the contingent dilution of the common stock equity is recognized in the Statement of Earnings as "Net Income—fully diluted."

STOCK DIVIDENDS AND STOCK SPLITS

Management may establish a policy of not declaring any cash dividends but rather declaring relatively frequent dividends payable in common stock or stock splits from time to time reflecting the retained earnings that are reinvested in the business for future growth. The reinvested earnings are thereby changed from retained earnings into capital (*i.e.*, common stock) that no longer can be used for paying cash dividends to stockholders. Such a procedure is an inexpensive method for a corporation to obtain funds for expansion and growth. If you own a growing company that uses this tack, it often results in an increase in the total market value of the original shares that you purchased. Some companies may pay small cash dividends but may, when circumstances permit and when the market price has increased sufficiently, declare a major stock dividend or a stock split.

In evaluating your stock, you should give favorable cognizance to this practice. Your earnings from the investment are a combination of the cash dividends plus the steady increase in the market value of the stock. Such market price increase is often recognized by the board of directors through the stock split or large dividend payable in common stock. As far as you are concerned, there is no difference between a stock split and a stock dividend. The difference is within the company and its accounting treatment.

REPURCHASE OF COMPANY STOCK

In considering the effectiveness of management with respect to repurchase of company stock, there are two schools of thought.

The management of a company with excess cash whose common stock is selling on the open market at less than the book value would purchase common stock, thereby increasing the book value and the equity of those stockholders who continue to own the common stock. For example, the management of company X may think that the purchase of its own stock may be the best investment it could make, thereby reducing the total cash outlay for quarterly dividends. The market value of the common stock of a company is $50 per share and the book value is $40 per share. The company purchases 100,000 shares at a cost of $5 million and cancels the stock having a book value of $4 million, thereby increasing retained earnings and the book value of the remaining outstanding shares by $1 million. It also increases the future earnings per share because there are 100,000 shares less outstanding. Assuming the company has been paying $1 per share cash dividends each quarter, it has reduced its dividend payment by $400,000 per year. The board of directors in making this decision decided that its own stock was its best investment. I'll let you make your own decision about this.

Another reason for making such purchases is to provide shares of stock for officers' and employees' stock options, and for issuing stock against stock warrants that could be exercised at a future date. Such stock purchased and held for possible reissue is called Treasury Stock.

Accumulating a fund of Treasury Stock to be used for the acquisition of new enterprises in a transaction involving the exchange of common stock for the common stock of the selling company may be advantageous. If your company has such a plan, it would not be necessary for it to issue unissued stock for such acquisitions.

In a smaller company, management might purchase outstanding stock that can be acquired below book value to improve the equity of the continuing stockholders. If the company is controlled by a small group of stockholders, it does enhance their percentage equity as against the non-insider stockholders. Furthermore, this may lead toward the possibility of making a tender offer for the balance of the stock and making the company a private company with the major stockholders in complete control.

What I am trying to point out is that you should try to put yourself in the position of the management as you read the annual report and try to imagine what management's objectives may be, based upon the various transactions and the way in which it deals with such matters.

MANAGEMENT POLICY DISCLOSURES

Stock repurchase transactions must be reported to the SEC and to the public. Management usually says very little about its intentions and very little about the policy it has established, but suddenly something happens. Then the intentions become public knowledge, but it might be too late for you to act.

Other companies may make a fixed policy that they will pay dividends of 40 percent to 50 percent of current earnings, and since this is an expressed policy it is good to know if there is a sudden change in the dividend rate.

DEFENSE AGAINST UNDESIRABLE POLICIES

One of the questions that could enter your mind as a stockholder is: "What defense do I have against actions that I don't like?" It is fair to state that there is very little that you can do. Of course, if you don't like how management runs the company, the best thing to do is sell the stock.

Efforts to change management's minds or upset management by stockholders' committees have not been too successful. There have been cases where management has been ousted by such a group, but this is usually done by a group of large stockholders joining together to upset management and take control of the company for their own benefit. Stockholders' actions against management usually result in a proxy fight and are costly, not only to the people who initiate them but also to the company that tries to defend them.

I suggest that as the average small stockholder, owning a few hundred shares, you study the plans and the materials submitted to you by both groups and then decide whether to remain with the company management, join the dissenters, or sell your stock. This is a business judgment that only you can make. Just bear in mind that as a stockholder you have an aliquot portion of the ownership and the same ratio of vote that is such a small percentage that no matter how democratic the company is run, your voice will be a very quiet whisper that may or may not be listened to by the winner.

9

Money

A business enterprise, whether industrial, commercial, wholesale, retail, service, or any other type, must begin with people whose contribution can be measured in man-hours but whose contribution of ideas has no unit of measurement.

The people need a place to perform their activities. This could be rented space or purchased space and is often measured in square feet.

The tools required could consist of a great variety of things such as furniture, fixtures, machinery, equipment transportation units, and many others with varied units of measure (horsepower, watts, amperes, yield, *etc.*) that may or may not be compatible.

The people buy many kinds of products that they use to create other products or services for sale to customers. Depending upon the nature of the purchases, they may be measured in ounces, pounds, hundred weight, tons, pints, quarts, gallons, and other forms of physical measurement.

The things and services they sell can also be accounted for in a great variety of measurements. I can go on at great length to describe the many units or quantities available and sometimes used. By now you should get some idea what I am driving at.

Putting all these measurements together would result in a hodge-podge of numbers that have no meaning and cannot be combined. But there is a better way.

Each item that is purchased, sold, rented, or used or represents work done, or service rendered can be measured by one uniform unit— dollars and cents. In other words, that artificial, standard medium of exchange, *money*.

It is money that makes the wheels go around and enables us to make comparisons. Among other things it enables us to establish an accounting system, without which a business enterprise could not function. From the accounting system, which serves many management purposes, we can derive financial statements that report, in summary form, the results of all of the many activities of the business enterprise during a specified period of time and the financial position of the enterprise at a date.

It is the purpose of this chapter to explain those financial statements that are included in the annual report to stockholders. Before you go any farther, get the most recent annual report of the company whose stock is your favorite investment. As you read further in this chapter, follow the suggestions I make and read that part of the financial statements and see how much more you will know about your company.

The name of the game for management is to make money. Management wants to make money because it is a measurement of its success. Management wants to make money:

- to pay dividends at an increasing rate to the stockholders
- to make the company grow
- to buy machinery and equipment for improved efficiency and growth
- to attract good management executives
- to improve executives' income through the effectiveness of the bonus plans and other executive incentives
- for the many things needed to operate a successful business with improving profits and growth potential.

Before examining any financial statements, read the auditors' report or at least look at it to make sure that it is the standard report with no variations. Reference should be made to Chapter 4, in which I discuss the significance of the report and what to look for. A quick glance will tell you whether you should scrutinize any particular part of the financial statements carefully and thoroughly.

The following discusses the financial statements in the annual report and how to interpret them.

STATEMENT OF EARNINGS

When you buy a security, you are interested principally in the earning power of the company and how this could be reflected in the market price of the securities—by common stock, preferred stock, and bonds. Hence many investors talk about the price/earnings ratio, which is the relationship of the market price of a share of common stock to the annual income per share resulting from the operations of the company. In other words, how many dollars you must pay to buy one dollar's worth of corporate income.

If a stock sells at a price/earnings ratio of six, it would require $6 to acquire one dollar's worth of earnings, and accordingly, if the total earnings were $1.50 per share, the market price of a share would be $9. Assuming that the company prospers and earnings increase to $2 per share, there are no other circumstances that could affect the market price and that the price/earnings ratio remains at six, the price for a share should go up to $12 per share. This is one of the reasons why the Statement of Earnings is such an important financial statement and why the average stockholder should become familiar with it.

The Statement of Earnings for a period (month, quarter year, or year), standing by itself, is not very meaningful. Unless you have some frame of reference and can relate this statement to other data, you cannot arrive at any real investment conclusion. Statements of Earnings in summary form are usually submitted to stockholders for interim periods of a quarter of a year that are not audited by the CPA. The SEC requires that annual reports are mailed before the annual stockholders' meeting with the financial statements audited by the independent CPA.

"RESULTS IN BRIEF"

Many hours could be spent analyzing the Statements of Earnings, but this cannot be done too effectively unless you have had accounting knowledge or stock analyst's experience and have read some of the many volumes that describe how to analyze financial statements. In order to make life easier for you, most companies have a section in their annual report called "Results in Bief," "Five-Year Summary," or "Ten-year Summary" that lists the most significant line items and compares them for a number of years. Furthermore, these summaries include the most important supplemental information, such as ratios, statistical data, and per share data, thereby avoiding the necessity of your making computations. Some of the more significant items that may be reported are:

Earnings and dividends
    Sales and other revenues
    Cost of sales
    Selling, general, and administrative expenses
    Income before income taxes and extraordinary items
    Provision for income taxes
    Net income
    Total dividends
Share data
    Average number of shares outstanding or number
      of shares used for per share computations
    Primary earnings per share
    Fully diluted earnings per share
    Dividends per common share
    Book value per common share
Balance sheet data
    Current assets
    Current liabilities
    Working capital
    Property, plant, and equipment
    Accumulated depreciation
    Long-term debt
    Stockholders' equity
Supplemental information and other data
    Net income as a percent of average
      stockholder's equity
    Net income as a percent of sales
    Allowance for depreciation
    Research and development expenditures
    Employees at year end
    Stockholders at year end

When management thinks that other disclosures will assist stockholders and others in evaluating its company, it may include them in this section. These could include such disclosures as volume statistics and investment per employee.

For you to understand these statements, the key is those numbers representing the per share data. For example, the bottom line of the Statement of Earnings frequently shows the earnings per common share. Scan these numbers to determine whether there has been a growth in earnings per share, because such growth would generally be reflected in the market price of the stock. The past is often the prologue for the future. A good rule of thumb could be that this number should increase by about 10 percent each year, which is an easy number to compute mentally. If there is a consistent increase in this number, you can assume that the favorable progress will continue (barring some unforeseen circumstances). Some consideration should be given to inflation in examining this line.

Another number that could be scanned very quickly is the top line, Revenues (or Sales). These amounts should significantly increase each year because such increases reflect the effect of volume increases, the effect of price increases, and the effect of inflation.

Some industries are able to report quantity statistics showing volume changes. Volume data are often reported by airlines in the form of passenger miles, by telephone companies by the number of telephones in service, by electric utilities on the basis of thousand of kilowatts or millions of kilowatt hours produced and sold, and so on. More time should be spent in examining the comparison of "Results in Brief" and the "ten-year summary" than the current-year detailed Statement of Earnings.

If the net earning per share or the sales and revenues are lower than in previous years, it then becomes important to determine the causes. This would frequently be discussed in the president's letter or in the "Management's Discussion and Analysis of Financial Condition and Results of Operations." It usually is a three-year comparison and discussion of those matters that influenced the net results. The format varies according to the industry and companies within an industry, so there is no normal pattern that can be discussed. Therefore, I suggest that you continue to read the management's discussions each year. Some are pretty dry reading at times, but interesting differences may stand out. It is the one place where management has the opportunity to say that this went wrong, or that this was especially good. Furthermore, it will give you some inkling of the caliber of management and its willingness to be candid and objective in disclosures to stockholders.

Another section that might be read at this point, or at least scanned, is the "Notes to the Financial Statements" to determine whether there are any subjects discussed therein that may have a direct bearing on the Statement of Earnings. The Notes to Financial Statements will be discussed in detail a little later in this chapter.

THE BALANCE SHEET

The Balance Sheet is the statement summarizing the tangible and intangible property that the company owns and the debt that it owes; the difference between the two is the book value of the stockholders' equity. The left side, called "assets," are the materials, property, and finances used by management to operate the company profitably so that you can receive dividends. The right side is what the company owes, liabilities, and stockholders' equity.

The assets are summarized as:

- Current assets, representing cash or other assets that can be converted into cash within the current operating cycle, which could be a year or less
- Investments that are long term and would probably be converted into cash only under unusual circumstances but contribute to the growth or stability of the company
- Property, plant, or equipment that is used to create the products sold or perform the services rendered. The cost of these assets will be charged to operating costs over the period of their useful life and must be replaced if the company is to continue as a successful operating company (see chapter 11)
- Other assets of various kinds that may be intangible, such as goodwill, the value of mineral rights, franchises, and other items.

The liabilities are summarized as:

- Current liabilities that must be paid within the yearly cycle
- Long-term debts of various kinds that must be paid off at a longer term and are due beyond a year from the date of the statement
- Stockholders' equity, which can consist of various classes of stock with different preferences (one must always be a common stock) Some companies may purchase or acquire their own common stock in the open market or through an unusual financial transaction. This stock, called Treasury Stock, is recorded at cost and is shown as a deduction from stockholders' equity. The Treasury Stock may be reissued (in most cases) at any time for any purpose as decided by the board of directors without a vote of the stockholders. It should not be confused with authorized but not issued stock, which can be issued only (in most instances) after a vote of the stockholders.
- Retained earnings (at one time called "surplus"). All dividends (other than liquidating dividends) are paid from retained earnings. Since the corporation is a separate entity from its stockholders, it could be considered that stockholders' equity is a permanent debt of the corporation to be paid only upon action by the board of directors who can authorize the payment in the form of dividends.

There are many ratios that have been developed and can be used in analyzing the balance sheet and its related statement of earnings. It is not the purpose of this book to discuss these fully because it is a technical subject for the evaluation of the company by the professional stock analysts. There will be an explanation of these ratios in Chapter 13. It is sufficient to say that you should compare the current year's amounts with the prior year's and if there is a large change for any particular item, try to find an explanation in the Notes to the Financial Statements or in the financial review of management accompanying the financial statements.

The ten-year financial summaries often include the more important line items of the balance sheet that usually make interesting reading. Some of these are:

- Book value per common share; this is derived by dividing the sum of the common stock, capital in excess of par value of capital stock (if any) and retained earnings, by the number of shares of common stock outstanding.
- Working capital, consisting of current assets less current liabilities. This is analyzed in detail in the Statement of Changes in Financial Position.
- Property, plant, and equipment and the related accumulated depreciation (see Chapter 11).
- Long-term debt.
- Stockholders' equity.

STATEMENT OF CHANGES IN STOCKHOLDERS' EQUITY

The "Statement of Changes in Stockholders' Equity" is a statement that is prepared more for the benefit of the professional analyst than for the average stockholder. It is required by the generally accepted auditing standard of reporting and is not very enlightening. The varied types of transactions that are reported in this statement are such that it would take a volume merely to go into them and, in many instances, would not be too significant for you. The highlights are (1) the dividends paid compared with the total net earnings and (2) to see whether there was any common stock purchased and retained as Treasury Stock during the reporting years. This is important only if the amounts involved are large in relation to the totals for the stock outstanding.

STATEMENT OF CHANGES IN FINANCIAL POSITION

The "Statement of Changes in Financial Position" is an interesting statement that is of significance to you particularly if there is a decreasing trend of working capital. The working capital change shown on the lower part of the statement consists of the net between the increases or decreases of current assets and of current liabilities. It may disclose a weakening in the financial position, which is a warning that should be heeded. Again, you should go to the Notes to Financial Statements or Management's Discussion to see if there are clues that explain what is going on.

Another step in your analysis is to examine the upper part of the statement. Compare the Sources of Working Capital with the Applications of Working Capital for a clue. Do likewise for prior years and compare the current year with the prior year. The reason for the adverse change may become evident. The questions that come to mind are:

Did the company spend a lot of money for fixed assets?
Did it buy Treasury Stock?
Did it invest in securities of another company?
Did it reduce the long-term debt?
Did the dividends paid exceed net earnings?
Did an operating loss have a material affect upon working capital?

You can apply your own good judgment about the importance of what has happened and the impact upon the future value of your investment.

There is one situation in which working capital could be reduced and yet foretell something about an improving future. The company may have been accumulating working capital for any of the purposes mentioned above. It would be reported in the section of the statement labeled "Application of Funds," which shows the amounts of money expended in excess of the sources of funds shown in the upper part of the statement. Again, the discussion of what causes this would be in the Management Review or in the Notes to Financial Statements.

NOTES TO FINANCIAL STATEMENTS

The Notes to Financial Statements are an integral and important part of the Financial Statements and should be scanned and, in some instances, read thoroughly.

The first part of these notes is usually a summary of significant accounting policies, such as:

- Principles of consolidation: reports the subsidiaries and companies owned and included in the financial statements.
- Translation of currency: If a company has foreign subsidiaries or foreign operations it must report how it translates the foreign currency into American currency.

- Inventory: the method of pricing inventory is important. There are two basic methods generally used: the first-in, first-out (FIFO), which is a technical phrase meaning that the pricing of inventories is such that the inventories on hand are assumed to be the most recent purchases and are priced accordingly. The other method is last-in, first-out (LIFO), meaning that the pricing of inventories assumes that the most recent purchases are charged to current operating costs. It is a tax-saving procedure, since the inventories are priced at the earliest purchases, usually at much lower prices than current cost; hence there is a deferred profit in the inventory and deferred federal income taxes results from this method. It should be considered that LIFO is the more conservative of the two methods, but there is no criticism of any company following either method to reflect its earnings. Under like conditions, a company using FIFO would show somewhat higher earnings than the same company using LIFO. Companies using LIFO for income tax purposes must use LIFO for financial-reporting purposes and must disclose the effect upon the inventory valuation and hence upon earnings. (See Chapter 10.)

- Property, depreciation, depletion, and amortization: fixed assets—principally machinery, furniture, and fixtures and equipment—are used up over a period of years because of wear and tear and obsolescence. Hence, a portion of the original cost must be applied to each year's earnings. This section discloses the methods for depreciation, amortization, and depletion (if applicable). It also includes the accounting principles followed for recording leases. There are many different rules and procedures for the accounting of fixed capital property and its related depreciation, depletion, and amortization, and for leases. It is pointless to say that this is a very technical subject and you cannot gain much by a thorough reading of this section. However, if time is available, comparisons can be made to see whether there were any major changes between the current year and the prior year. If this occurred, it would be reflected in the Management Discussion. (See Chapter 11.) This note also states the company's policy for capitalization as compared with charging replacements, repairs, and renewals against current earnings.

- Revenue recognition: this subject does not appear in all financial reports. It refers particularly to situations where the company performs long-term contracts such as construction of buildings and plants, large vessels, long-term government contracts, and the like. It is not easy to determine actually how much of the earnings is attributable to each fiscal period. In this event, arbitrary accounting policies are made and disclosed in this footnote.

- Income taxes: income from certain types of transactions are sometimes deferred and recognized in different years for financial-reporting purposes as compared with the treatment in the income tax returns. This approved procedure results in deferral of income tax payments. The differences are generally discussed in this section of the notes. It also describes how investment credits and foreign tax credits are handled. A short schedule usually reconciles the basic income tax rate with the net rate reflected in the financial statement, which is usually lower as the result of good corporate tax planning.

- Earnings per common share and common share equivalents: this note discloses the method of computation of earnings per share, the number of shares involved for each computation, and similar information. Again, it is a subject for use by the stock analyst, but sometimes it can disclose matters of interest to you. When applicable the company reports income from continuing operations and income or loss from discontinued operations. This usually results from the restructuring of the company's operations. Continuing operations are more pertinent for evaluation of potential future results. Occasionally you will find earnings per share reported as "fully diluted." This assumes that all stock options are exercised, all convertible securities are converted, and all warrants are exercised. The fully diluted amount is usually less than primary earnings per share, and the difference is generally not large or material in amount and therefore you need not be too concerned. Furthermore, the contingent transactions that are involved will occur over many years.

- Reclassifications: this is another item that is not included in all reports. It applies to changes in reported captions or transfers from one classification to another in either the Balance Sheet or the Statement of Earnings and is only for comparison purposes and therefore is not a very important matter.

- Long-term debt: this consists of arrangements in connection with the company's borrowings, bank loans, and such, which are disclosed in a note showing the due dates for long-term debts, that is of particular interest to you if a long-term debt is due in the near future and if the company has a financial problem that should be considered. For example, if a major final payment for a long-term debt with low interest rates is due in the next year or two, the company may have to go to the marketplace to borrow at current high rates. This could have an adverse effect upon future earnings.

- Quarterly earnings: of particular interest is the reporting of unaudited quarterly earnings. Most companies' earnings and revenues are fairly uniform throughout the fiscal year. Some companies and industries have seasonal differences in earning capacity. For example, energy companies have greater revenues in certain quarters than others; another example is in the textbook-publishing industries, where companies usually have losses or low income in certain quarters and large earnings in others. The most important earnings are for the full year.

There are many sections in the Notes to the Financial Statements disclosing details of items that appear in the Balance Sheet or Statement of Earnings. This is more for clarification and information and generally is not of major importance.

This brings to mind the statement previously made—that you must get to know your company and the peculiarities of its industry. Reading these financial statements and their notes will help in this regard.

The comments made here cover the more significant notes that appear frequently. The first time you read an annual report of a company you should read the notes fairly thoroughly so as to get acquainted and an understanding of them. Many of the notes are repeated year in and year out with updated amounts and minor changes. It is suggested that you get sufficiently familiar with the Notes to the Financial Statements so that you can pass by most of them that do not appear to have any new significance to you, are included because they are required by the rules, or can be used to a great extent by professional financial analysts. Underscore those notes that you think are important to identify those notes that you want to read when you get next year's report.

ISSUED DATES OF ANNUAL REPORTS

A word of caution about using the financial statements: Bear in mind that you receive annual reports from companies in which you own stock, even if you leave the stock in the broker's name, about two to three months *after* the date of the statements. If you get them later in the year, there might be an even greater lapse of time.

If you don't own the stock, you can get statements of companies that interest you merely by requesting them from the company or examining them at your broker's office or in your local library. Most local libraries do have reports of the larger, more active companies and companies in their area. But in any event, bear in mind that the financial statements are not the most recent financial information available.

More recent information is available at your broker's office, in the local papers and financial magazines, and from stock services. For most of the companies, the changes during short periods are so minor that it really has no great bearing upon any decision that you might make. However, unusual things that happen after the year's end may not be reflected in the financial statements that you have received and yet may have a direct bearing upon any decision that you might want to make now. So before taking the action, check with your broker to find out what, if anything, has occurred since the end of the last fiscal year's financial statements.

ANNUAL STOCKHOLDERS' MEETING

Another way to get an update on what has happened since the end of the year is to attend the stockholders' meeting of your company. The president usually makes prepared remarks about what has occurred since the annual statement, or about what is to be expected for the future. It is a good education in itself to listen to the president and to other officers, and to listen to the questions that are raised by other stockholders, some of whom have substantial investments in your company.

SUMMARY

If you own stock in a company, you will receive financial statements each year. It is worthwhile to retain copies for several years; I suggest a minimum of three to make some quick comparisons of the basic numbers and the basic comments made in the president's letter. It is interesting to note what the president said the future would hold and compare it with what the actual results were. Doing this can give you a good feeling of the management and how much confidence you might place in its disclosures.

Bear in mind that owning stock is a confidence game, but it's not the kind of confidence game that you usually think of. It's a game in which you have a high or a low degree of confidence in the management. If it's a low degree, get out. If it's a high degree, buy more or at least continue to hold what you now own. Remember that the management is using *your* money to run your business, and this is true whether you buy an original issue direct from the company or whether you buy the stock through a broker from former stockholders who have owned the stock for many years. The other stockholder is merely transferring his or her investment in the company to you through his or her sale and your purchase, so you have just as much at stake as if you had purchased the stock directly from the company at the time it was initially issued.

10

Materials
and Merchandise

Inventory is the life blood of a company. In one way or another, it flows through or affects all operations. It consists of materials and merchandise purchased, grown, or extracted from the soil that is then manufactured into something that is prepared for sale, packaged, and subsequently sold (we hope). If there isn't enough inventory of finished goods of the right kind, sales cannot be completed on time and customers could go elsewhere. Materials purchased for production must be of sufficient quantities; otherwise the finished products cannot be produced on time and efficiently in accordance with a production schedule prepared so that merchandise would be available for sale when needed.

PHYSICAL INVENTORY COUNTS

If there is too much inventory, working capital is needlessly frozen, and this could result in financial strains upon the company. Generally, inventories consist of raw materials (in the very broad sense), work in process, and finished goods. In some instances it also includes supplies that are consumed in the operations of the business (such as lubricants, fuel, housekeeping materials, etc.). Some companies find that it is a better policy to charge supplies to expense when acquired, eliminating some of the accounting and recordkeeping. Good inventory management is a highly technical subject that could add to efficient operation and profitable operating results.

Inventories must be counted periodically and valued for internal control purposes, cost accounting, and financial accounting and reporting. A good perpetual inventory system can be a substitute for the count, but it must be tested from time to time to assure its accuracy. The physical existence of the inventory must be established as of at least the end of the fiscal accounting year for testing in accordance with established auditing procedures by the independent auditors.

INVENTORY PRICING METHODS

Inventory is valued for presentation on the balance sheet, and for determining the result of operations.

There are two major methods of pricing inventories that you should be aware of and should understand. The principal GAAP is that the inventory is priced at lower of cost or market, generally referred to as first-in, first-out (FIFO). There are several accounting conventions pertaining to the lower of cost or market that are not of particular importance to you as an investor. However, just for the record, I will mention some of the more common ones. "Cost" is the actual cost of the units that are identified so that it represents those actually on hand. However, in many of the instances—such as pieces of steel or nuts and bolts—the purchase price of the particualr unit on hand is not available. The conventions are that they are priced at the basis of the most recent acquisitions, group pricing, or average pricing.

There is a very distinct method for pricing inventories of retail stores or department stores, naturally referred to as the "retail method." The details of this method are somewhat complex, and it is not important for the average investor to understand the method.

Work-in-process and manufactured finished goods are priced in accordance with the company's normal cost system. There are a great variety of cost systems, each tailor-made to the company's management's specific needs. The cost system is reviewed and tested by the independent auditor.

"Market" can generally be described as the cost, in the ordinary course of business, of replacing the inventory in like kind by purchase or reproduction.

The other major method was established some years ago by the Internal Revenue Service for determining income for tax returns, known as last in, first out (LIFO). This is also a permissible method for accounting purposes under GAAP. It is used by many companies to reduce current taxes, which are deferred indefinitely until the inventory quantity is reduced or is completely used up. For those using LIFO, the IRS and the SEC have established certain strict rules and regulations. They are:

- You cannot change from LIFO to any other method without IRS permission.
- You must use LIFO for financial reporting purposes.
- You must report the difference between LIFO and FIFO at the beginning and end of each year in the financial statements, usually in the notes.

Some companies explain the effect that LIFO has upon cost of sales, stating, in essence, that it is a better matching of current cost with revenues and the inventory profits are eliminated from inventory. This recognizes the effect of inflation and hence is a more conservative method of reporting. The basic principle of LIFO is that the current income is better determined by deducting from sales of the period the cost of replacing the merchandise used or sold. It assumes that the sales are the most recent acquisitions. Whether it is produced or purchased, it is charged to operations at current costs.

You need not concern yourself about which method is used, since from an investor's viewpoint it does not have any material significance. However, I've explained the two methods for your information because FIFO and LIFO are often used in the text and in notes to the financial statements in the annual reports without a clear definition.

INVENTORY FOR LONG-TERM CONTRACTS

Another inventory item of interest is the accounting for long-term contracts, whether with the government or with other companies for large items that require several years to perform. These could be the construction of a ship, the manufacture of a quantity of railroad cars, or a major construction contracted. The work in progress would consist of units in various stages of production at the end of each accounting period. The method followed is often described in the note on principal accounting policies as "Inventory costs relating to long-term contracts are stated at the actual production cost incurred to date, reduced by progress payments received. The costs attributable to units delivered under such contracts are based on the estimated average cost of all units expected to be produced.''

This should not be of any great concern to you since you can rest assured that the independent auditor has examined the pricing under these various methods, where attributable and found them satisfactory for the purpose according to GAAP.

HOW TO REVIEW INVENTORIES REPORTED

What should interest you as a stockholder is the size of the inventory as reported in the balance sheet. One clue that a company may be in financial trouble is an excessive inventory—but this is not always the case.

The usual term used in expressing inventory relationships is *turnover*. This term refers to the frequency with which the inventory is disposed of and replaced within the year. It is determined by dividing the cost of goods sold by the average amount of inventory. Depending upon the nature of the business, this could vary greatly. As an investor, you should try to get some idea what the inventory turnover is in the type of business you are considering. A turnover of five or six times a year is not unreasonable. If the number is much less than that, one reason may be the nature of the business, in that the lenght of time from acquisition of the raw material to the final production of finished goods is long, such as in the heavy construction business. What may be something to worry about is that the inventory may contain a large amount of nonsalable, obsolete merchandise. In accordance with GAAP, such inventory should be valued at its salable value (which is less than cost) or written off entirely and the loss recognized in the earnings statement as soon as it is determined, which is in accordance with the concept of the lower of cost or market.

SUMMARY

It is rather difficult, in examining the figures made available in an annual report, to come to any sound conclusions about the management of inventories. While inventory may not be the largest asset on the balance sheet, it is very fluid and constantly changing. It might be desirable to compare the inventories for the last three years (which are the only amounts usually available in the financial statements submitted) with the sales for each of these years. A significant change upwards might result from the company's going into a new major product. A significant change downward may be the result of liquidation of a plant or an operation. If there is a significant change, try to determine from other data in the annual report whether there is a reason that can be ascertained, or whether management, in one of its letters or in one of the notes, makes an explanation.

11

Machinery and Equipment

The previous chapter discussed inventories, a very fluid and constantly changing asset. This chapter discusses machinery and equipment, or, as they are often called, fixed assets, because the changes in their status are usually sporadic and relatively slow. This information on the balance sheet goes by a variety of names, such as "Plant, machinery, and equipment," "Fixed assets," and "Property, plant, and equiment" and includes but is not limited to land, natural resources, buildings, machinery and equipment, automobiles, and furniture and fixtures. It is an asset that is vital to the company.

FIXED ASSETS AND DEPRECIATION

As a general rule, there are additions to these fixed assets each year in modest amounts. Periodically there is a major addition, either to increase the scope or amount of production, to replace inefficient and obsolete machinery, or for one of the many reasons that management has for making such expenditures.

Cumulative reduction in amount by normal usage is reported as depreciation, depletion, and amortization (hereafter referred to collectively as depreciation). Sale, abandonment, or other disposition is accounted for by reduction of the asset and elimination of the accumulated depreciation. The gain or loss, if any, is reported in the statement of earnings, and if material in amount, as an extraordinary item. Such a transaction occurs infrequently.

The total amount invested in fixed assets and still owned by the company is shown in the balance sheet. The amount of money spent to acquire fixed assets within the particular accounting period would appear in the Statement of Changes in Financial Position under the label "Uses of Funds" or under the caption "Appication of Working Capital" as "Additions to Property, Plant, and Equipment" or a similar phrase depending upon the preference of the company, its management, or their auditors.

DEPRECIATION, DEPLETION, AND AMORTIZATION

Fixed assets are consumed very slowly by the passage of time, by the use for the production of goods, or for any other purpose for which they were acquired. The accounting for these uses is reported in the financial statements as a charge against income and as a reduction of the net asset value on the balance sheet. The deduction from the balance-sheet item is frequently called "Less accumulated depreciation" or some similar phraseology and shown separately, thereby retaining the accounting and reporting of the original cost. The amount of depreciation is not always shown separately on the statement of earnings, but it frequently is shown in the ten-year financial summaries, and it always appears on the Statement of Changes and Financial Position under the caption "Charges to income not requiring the use of funds."

INCOME TAX CONSEQUENCES

There are many accounting conventions on how to charge a portion of the original cost against each year's earnings.

The company may choose between an appropriate charge for financial purposes, which may be different from that allowable for income tax purposes. There are a number of accelerated depreciation and depletion charges that reduce current taxes, and it behooves the company to take advantage of them. If that is done, the company discloses the fact in the text of the note to financial statements pertaining to income taxes where they report the difference between the taxable income and income reported on the financial statements. This difference results from the use of accelerated cost recovery methods for tax purposes that might provide more depreciation in the earlier years of the ownership than in the latter years. The total amount deducted over the years cannot exceed the original cost.

This treatment is often referred to as a timing difference in that the deduction from gross earnings is taken in a different time frame (usually earlier) for tax purposes or in a greater amount than it is for financial purposes. Such difference in timing can make a significant difference in the effective tax rate for a particular year as compared with other companies. It really is not a very significant amount of dollars in relation to the financial planning of a company, but it is interesting to note that many companies do take advantage of tax-deferral provisions.

DEPRECIATION METHODS

I cannot go into a discussion of each and every major depreciation method and rate, since it is not the purpose of this book to get into such detail. That is more important to security analysts, accountants, and professionals than to the average stockholder. None of these depreciation variations should have any influence upon your decision to buy, sell, or hold a stock.

For your information purposes, depreciation is a procedure based upon the number of years of useful life of the fixed assets, whereby the total cost of the asset is charged against gross income so that, when the equipment is obsolete, worn out, or otherwise no longer useful, the balance on the books merely represents salvage value.

Amortization of some fixed assets may represent the allocation of the cost over a period of years not necessarily reflecting its useful life. An example is leasehold improvements, which might have a longer useful life than the term of the lease but are amortized over the shorter term because their usefulness to the company relates to the lease period.

Depletion is the term used for accounting of the reduction value (which is even more complex) of natural resources, a form of fixed assets, such as coal, oil, minerals, and natural gas. The original cost of acquiring the property and developing it to a useful state is recorded as a fixed asset and is amortized as depletion. During the development of the property, an estimate is made of the total available quantity of the natural resource. A unit cost is computed based upon the total cost of acquisition and development of the property and the estimated quantity expected to be recovered. Each year, the amount of natural resource removed is priced at that unit, and the resulting amount is the depletion charged against income and reduces the asset. From time to time, the estimated quantity may be changed as additional quantities are discovered and as new development costs are incurred. This is a simplified discussion of the general method. There are many variations, depending upon the types of natural resources and the policies established by the company.

It is important to note that the policies and methods are consistently followed. If a change is made, it usually is mentioned in the Notes to Financial Statements.

The depreciation, depletion, or amortization of fixed assets is established by management's policy and is generally described in some detail in the accounting principles in the Notes to the Financial Statements. Even companies that have no product to sell (service companies) may have substantial amounts of fixed assets. For example, The American Telephone and Telegraph Company (before divestiture) furnished a communication service. Yet, upon looking at the balance sheet you would find that its telephone plant at cost, less accumulated depreciation, represents more than 85 percent of the total assets. A similar situation exists for separated telephone companies. The ratio of plant, machinery, and equipment to total assets for manufacturing companies generally varies considerably. It is not unusual to find that net fixed assets, the original cost less the accumulated depreciation, is frequently in the range of 50 percent of its total assets.

COMPARING ACCUMULATED DEPRECIATION WITH ORIGINAL COST

It is interesting to note the original cost of the fixed asset and compare it with accumulated depreciation. If the accumulated depreciation exceeds 50 percent of the original cost, there might be reason for concern. It depends upon the nature of the business and policy of the company for charging fixed assets to current costs at an accelerated depreciation rate within the GAAP.

If the normal straight-line method or a variation of it is used, the large accumulated depreciation amount might imply that the plant is approaching a point where a good portion of the property may be obsolete or may require replacement. It might indicate that the equipment may be old and therefore not as effficient as newer equipment. It might imply that the company may have to make some substantial cash expenditures to replace the aging plant.

In examining the fixed aseets situation in a company it appears appropriate to examine the Statement of Changes in Financial Position to determine the amount of additions to property plant and equipment during recent years and compare it with the depreciation for the same years. This could give some indication as to management's viewpoint about managing this very imporant asset. If the new additions are consistently less than the depreciation, there could be cause for concern.

FINANCING FIXED ASSETS

Companies may go into the public marketplace and issue bonds for the acquisition of fixed assets, or it may purchase a building with a significant mortgage whereby the amortization of the debt is related to the life of the asset purchased. The amortization or repayment of the debt should be of a shorter period than the depreciation write-off for the assets acquired so that at the end there can be a positive cash flow improving the financial position of the company and provide cash for the higher cost of the replacement due to inflation.

LEASES

Some companies acquire a portion of their fixed assets through leases. The amounts usually are disclosed in the financial reports. There are two kinds of leases. One is "capital lease," which is the equivalent of purchasing the asset on the installment basis. These leases usually have a provision that the company can buy the assets at the end of the lease term or the term can be extended approaching the useful life. These leases are, in essence, a form of financing the acquisition of fixed assets.

Other leases, such as leasing a floor in an office building, leasing a computer, or leasing a building for a limited period of time with no provision for the acquisition of the property at the end of the lease, are generally referred to as operating leases.

Capital leases are recorded on the financial statements as if the company acquired the assets for a cost that represents the present value of the series of lease payments. This again is a technical subject and need not concern you too much. If the numbers are large, the subject is discussed at length in the Notes to the Financial Statements. Read them.

The cost of acquiring property for use through leases can be more expensive than owning such assets. However, there are many reasons why a company might do this. One is the need for cash and future cash flow. Another is the maintenance of the equipment. This might be particularly true for the acquisition of computers or of a fleet of trucks or automobiles with an operating lease so that the company need not concern itself with these unusual costs. Another reason for leasing might be that the asset leased is highly technical equipment and the changes in the technology are frequent. In such a case the company might then want to update its equipment frequently before the equipment becomes physically worn out. In that event leasing may be less costly than purchasing.

SUMMARY

It is evident from the discussion here that the manner in which a company acquires its important fixed assets might be indicative of the management's concern for the welfare of the stockholders. Should it put stockholders' money into bricks, mortar, steel, metals, and machinery or shall it use the available resources for running the company by spending it for intangibles that create income and do not require as much frozen capital as owning plants, warehouses, and shopping malls? You should give consideration to the nature of the business and to the results of the policies established by the company for its operations and decide whether you feel that management is doing the best thing for you before you become a part owner of the company.

12

Markets

It is good to know how your company markets its products. Does it have a few very large customers or many small and medium-sized ones? Does it sell its products to one or two selected industries or does it sell to a great variety of industries? Does it advertise its products and services in such a way that it can attract new customers? Does it sell directly to the public or does it sell through agencies, wholesalers, franchisees, or retailers?

It is hard to get the answers to these questions from the annual report. Some companies spell out in great detail what their products are and to what sector of the markets they try to sell them. This information can generally be ascertained from the listing of their product lines in the annual report.

SEGMENT REPORTING

One place that you can get an idea of what's going on in this field is in the report on business segments in the Notes to the Financial Statements. These segments are usually pretty broad, but they give some sort of an idea as to whether the segments are related or not. It also gives some clues as to whether the companies sell principally to wholesalers, to other manufacturers, or to retailers. I am not trying to say that one is better than the other; I am merely pointing out that you should evaluate this in the light of what you want in the companies that you invest in.

Segment reporting also requires that the company disclose the extent of its foreign trade. It should be recognized that in some parts of the world dealing with foreign governments or companies in emerging countries could be risker than dealing in the United States. In addition to the sales prospects there is always the problem of monetary exchanges and currency translations. On the other hand, dealing in these contries can be very lucrative in spite of the risks involved.

FORM 10-K

The company files Form 10-K annually with the SEC. Among other things, this includes a section on markets. If you are interested in this phase of your company's operation you can get a copy of Form 10-K from the company by making a request to the officer indicated in the annual report. It is good to get this in any event, because it expands on some of the information that is in the annual report.

MANAGEMENT OF MARKETING

It is also desirable to see how important the marketing element is in the company in which you invest. If it is given a very high ranking by its management scheme of things it frequently appoints one or more marketing vice presidents. This is usually a good sign.

In reading the biographies of the chairman of the board, president, and other inside members of the board of directors, it is interesting to note through what phase of operation the individuals advanced in the company. If they advanced through sales promotion or marketing, it is evident that marketing ranks high in the management view. In your daily life you can observe much about the marketing of your company's products. If it sells consumer goods, observe its advertising and its displays in supermarkets, chain stores, and department stores; if it serves fast foods, try them; if it sells industrial products, look for its advertisements in newspapers, business magazines, or weekly news magazines; keep your eyes open for its products wherever they are used. I first decided to examine the financial aspects of a potential investment from observing its products and ads. Some of these investments turned out pretty well.

There is little more that I can say about how you can examine the marketing operations of your investments. However, what little you can learn should add to your fund of knowledge.

13

Financial
and Investment Ratios

THE PURPOSE OF THIS CHAPTER

Many books and articles have been written about financial ratios and business ratios—how they are computed, how they are used, and what decisions can be made based upon them. Investment analysts use many ratios because they must give an opinion in depth on all types of investments and must report information from their findings to all kinds of investors from the rank amateur to the highly sophisticated managers of large portfolios. It is my intention to cover only those ratios that are of sufficient importance for the average investor to use in an investment decisions. It is also my intention to discuss only those ratios that appear in the annual report and, in a number of instances, that appear in the daily newspapers and investors magazines.

It will not be necessary to be able to compute a ratio if you know what it means and how to use it for your investment programs. Knowledge of how ratios are computed might help, but it is not essential. Therefore, if you want to understand the background and the computation of the ratios discussed, there is information in Appendix E explaining the basic mathematical concepts.

Most of the ratios can be easily computed with pencil and paper or with a simple pocket calculator. If you really want to get into this subject in depth, there are many books that you can get from the library, and if you own or have access to a microcomputer you can get appropriate software and really go to town.

DEFINITION OF A RATIO

A ratio usually is a simple number of one, two or three digits, perhaps with a decimal point and one digit after the decimal point. It could also be a relationship between two numbers, such as 2 to 1. These can be used for judgment purposes, but there must be a name identifying the ratio. It is generally used as a comparison between another, similar ratio or number, such as for a prior period, an established goal, or the same ratio in another company.

The word *ratio* is defined in *Webster's New World Dictionary of the American Language, Second College Edition*, as follows:

1. A fixed relation in degree, number, etc. between two similar things; proportion (a ratio of two boys to three girls).
2. *Finance:* the relative value of gold and silver in a currency system based on both.
3. *Math:* the quotient of one quantity divided by another of the same kind, usually expressed as a fraction.

I hope this hasn't confused you. If I were to wrrite my own definition, I would say that a ratio is a simple number, fraction, or numerical relationship that can be compared with a similar number that is:

1. a target or goal
2. computed for a budget
3. computed for prior periods
4. computed for other companies
5. considered manual, standard, or desirable
6. helpful to make a decision.

HOW RATIOS ARE USED

Get out your *Wall Street Journal, New York Times,* or local newspaper and look for the New York Stock Exchange—Composite Transactions and study it briefly. In addition to the fifty-two-week high and low, the quantity and prices, you will see three very important columns: *Div* (dividend paid), *Yield %* (the income earned expressed as a percentage that the dividend earns on the closing market price), and *P/E Ratio* (the price/earnings ratio, which will be explained more fully later). The *Yield %* and the *P/E Ratio* are probably the two ratios considered most important and are used most frequently by investors.

For example, the ratio most commonly used and referred to is the P/E Ratio. In reading your daily quotations, you see the P/E Ratio of the particular stock is 9. You may have decided not to buy any stock in certain industries unless the P/E Ratio is under 10. That is the comparison of the daily ratio with a ratio you have in mind. Another use is to compare the P/E Ratio as published with a similar ratio of other companies in the same industry.

In recent years, stockholders' annual reports include most important ratios as encouraged by the SEC and the stock exchanges. Hence, to a great extent stockholders need not make a computation of any major ratio because the work is done for them, and a comparison is also made between years. Stockbrokers who issue news items about companies for their customers and the many financial publications that write about specific issues, such as Standard & Poor's, Moody's, Value Line, and others, usually include ratios in their articles that are all helpful to the investor knowledgeable on this subject. I will discuss each of the more common ratios in the following paragraphs, indicating what they mean and how they can be used for investment decisions.

As a word of caution, note that each company computes its ratios but may use slightly different procedures from those of other companies. In most instances, these differences are not important and cannot be found unless you do very thorough research and have access to some of the details. Just remember that this is not as exact science.

PRICE/EARNINGS RATIO (P/E)

The Price/Earnings Ratio is probably the most frequently mentioned and discussed ratio in any conversation among investors, between investors and their stockbrokers, and in the literature. It represents a single number that relates the current market price of the stock to the company's yearly earnings per share ("earnings per share" is a ratio discussed later). What it represents is the number of years of annual earnings of a company required to purchase one share of stock. It also represents the number of dollars one must pay to buy one dollar of annual earnings. It never appears in an annual report because it can change from day to day.

For example, a stock that earns $2 per share and sells at ten times earnings, or $20, would have a P/E Ratio of 10. If the earnings go up to $2.20 and the market still equates this company as being worth ten times earnings, the market price would go up to $22. On the other hand, if the marketplace thinks that the value of the stock of this company, because of future prospects, an anticipated merger, or any one of the many things that could change the price of a stock, bids the price up to $22 but the earnings remain at $2 per share, the stock is said to sell eleven times earnings, or a P/E Ratio of 11.

Since the P/E Ratio is 10 and the earnings per share is $2 and since $10 will buy $1 of earnings, the market price would be $20. Similarly, if the earnings per share is $2.20, the market for the stock would go up to $22 if everything else is equal.

There are two principal ways in which you can read this ratio. It can be compared with the P/E Ratio sometimes reported in news articles of the market as a whole, determined by a computerized figure of the P/E Ratio of the Dow Jones average based on the statistical amount of the earnings of the stocks that constitute that average. This is one way to compare the P/E Ratio of a specific stock with the market as a whole.

On the other hand, a more common use is to compare the P/E Ratio of another company in the same or similar industry with the stock you are interested in. A decision to buy, sell, or hold your particular stock may depend upon your view of the current P/E Ratio. Bear in mind that it represents the relationship of two of the most important factors in investment decisions, namely, how much each share of stock earns and the market price of that stock on the current market auctions.

There often may be a time lag between good or bad news about a company and a corresponding change in the P/E Ratio. For example, the company may announce that the next quarter's earnings will be much higher than current earnings. Not until the actual amount is reported and reflected in the twelve-months earnings that is the denominator of the computation will the game of catch-up be completed. Bear this time lag in mind when using this ratio.

For an example, see Chapter 7, where I compare GTE with AT&T.

YIELD

The yield of a particular stock is the relationship between the current dividend rate to today's market price. It represents a percentage and is frequently quoted in one or two digits. If the yield is less than 10 percent, it could be quoted in two digits with a decimal point.

For example, given a stock that pays an annual dividend of $1 per share and the market price is $20, the yield is 5 percent and, accordingly, it would be reported in the newspapers at just 5. If the price goes up to $22 the yield would be reported as 4.6. As the price of the stock goes down and the dividend remains fixed, the yield goes up; and conversely, if the price of the stock goes up, the yield goes down. If you are interested in income as well as the market price of your stock, this is an important ratio.

Hence, if you want to have income in excess of, let us say, 6 percent, you might find that you would have to look into certain industries where the dividends are high and where they normally exceed 6 percent. Mature companies in a mature industry often sell in the marketplace more on the basis of the yield than the P/E Ratio, although there is often a relationship between the two. It is important for you to watch these two ratios and compare them.

If the P/E Ratio goes up and continues to go up, this could be caused by the market price's going up or the earnings' going down, or a combination of both. If there has been no significant change in earnings per share, the increase in P/E can be due to increased market prices resulting from a number of factors, such as a general rise in the market, favorable rumors or other factors that indicate future gains in the company, possible mergers or tender offers, the industry's being looked upon favorably, and others too numerous to mention.

However, if the market price has been stable but earnings per share are declining, there is the possibility that the company may reduce its quarterly dividends and thus the price of the stock may go down.

If the P/E is declining, it could be caused by the market price's going down or the earning's going up, or a combination. This may be an opportunity for an increase in the dividend that would increase the yield on an investment and cause the price of the stock to go up. However, the reducing P/E Ratio may be anticipating some bad news about your company, and it might be time to sell your stock and avoid further losses. At some point in time, this relationship may dictate to you that it is time to sell the stock and take advantage of the capital gain, or to buy more stock for future gains.

EARNINGS PER SHARE

Earnings per share is in fact a ratio expressed in dollars and cents. It is a component of the P/E Ratio. You will find it in news items and in periodicals about stocks. You will find it in news items representing the quarterly release of earnings by the company, in material furnished by your stockbrokers, in articles in magazines, and, last but not least, in the annual report. It usually is shown as the last item on the statement of earnings (as is required by GAAS), which is always comparative for two or three years. You will also find the earnings per share in the five- or ten-years summaries, where you can follow the trend of the earnings per share so that you can measure the growth of the company and the stability of its earnings (sometimes referred to as "quality of earnings"). It is much easier looking at this one number as an amount you can understand because you can look in your pocket and see what $2.35 per share means in currency. This is what you are buying when you buy a share of stock, and, if you own 300 shares, you can multiply the earnings per share by 300 and determine your part of the company's earnings. This is one factor, among many others, that influence the market price of the stock.

You can also compare this with the dividend yield. It is interesting to note the portion of each year's earnings that is distributed to the owners (the stockholders). (See later in this chaper on "Dividend payout.")

"Earnings per share" pertains to earnings per common share and frequently refers to "primary earnings" and "fully diluted earnings." An explanation of how these two numbers are computed is usually included in the Notes to Financial Statements as a separate note or in Note 1—Principal Accounting Policies. Fully diluted earnings are usually less than primary earnings. "Fully diluted earnings per share" is an artificial number assuming that all convertible securities (bonds and/or preferred stocks) are converted into common stock, all options and warrants are exercised, and similar obligation requiring the issuance of common stock are completed. The difference between primary and fully diluted earnings per share is usually small, and accordingly you should rely on the primary earnings for your conclusions. Those amounts are factual, whereas fully diluted involves many contingencies.

I have now discussed three most important ratios that should influence stockholders in their decisions. However, the other ratios I am going to discuss in the following paragraphs are also important and you should know about them. They contribute much to your knowledge.

RETURN ON EQUITY

There are basically two kinds of ratios: those that pertain to earnings of the company and those that pertain to the financial stability of the company as reflected in the balance sheet. Return on equity is the last of the income-type ratios that I will discuss.

This ratio represents the relationship between the earnings of the company as reflected by the bottom line of the statement of earnings to the total investment made in the company by all its stockholders as represented by the capital stock, both common and preferred, and its retained earnings. There are variations of the computations of this ratio. In some instances, there are long-term debt and other equity items included.

The return on equity really represents a percentage. A simple example may clarify this. Suppose you started a business with $100,000 and throughout the years the company earned money that you reinvested by not taking it out in the form of dividends. Let us assume that this amount is $50,000. Therefore, the total equity as of a specific date would be $150,000. Let's assume that the earnings of your business after income tax—in other words, the bottom line for the current year—are $15,000. Therefore, the business has given you a return of 10 percent on equity in the business. This is what is meant when return on equity is reported in the annual report, usually in the five- or ten-year summary.

Not all companies report this number, but it is an interesting number to look at for those companies that do report it. As a word of caution, there is a difference between the methods used for computing the return on equity between companies that is not disclosed in the annual reports and usually cannot be determined without doing a bit of research. This comes about through the determination of the denominator of the fraction used to compute this ratio. In some instances, items are included in the denominator that require a change in the numerator, but these variations are not too significant on an overall basis. Some companies use the equity amounts for the end of the year; others average the amounts for the beginning and the end of the year. The latter procedure is the more desirable and the one used by most of the companies.

There are two ways in which this ratio can be used. The first is principally as a comparison between years that should show no great variations. If the ratio gradually gets higher, it could be because the company is utilizing its assets more efficiently, operating at a more profitable rate, increasing revenues and sales without a similar increase in capital investment, or for other similar reasons. It reflects good management. If the ratio goes down, something may be wrong. Look in the management report section for an explanation.

The other way is a comparison between companies in the same industry to see how effectively management is using the capital that you have entrusted to them for making profits and improving your investments.

If this ratio is substantially different from that of most companies in the same industry, it may be that your company computes it differently. Another cause might be a different capital structure. The cause of this difference might be difficult to track down. If you are considering investing in a certain industry it might be wise to invest in the company with the highest return on equity.

RESEARCH AND DEVELOPMENT TO SALES

"Research and Development to Sales" is a specialized ratio. Certain industries in high technological fields, such as those of electronics, computers, drugs, and chemicals, spend considerable funds on developing new products, improving old products, increasing plant efficiencies, and improving the utilization of manpower. Research and Development (R & D) is an expense that can be controlled by management through budgetary and control techniques. The amount of expenditures, while partially influenced by outside factors, can be increased or decreased pretty much by a policy decision of top management.

The number is a percentage that represents the amount of revenues from sales that are allocated to R & D and usually ranges between 3 and 10 percent of those companies that report these data. Some companies report the dollar amount of R & D in the five- or ten-year summaries. Other companies refer to it in the president's letter, in the management report, or in the Notes to the Financial Statements or show the dollar amount and the corresponding percentage separately in their statement of earnings. You might have to dig a little into the annual report to find it. In any event, it is an interesting amount to look at if it is available to you. It reflects the extent to which the company is trying to develop new sources of income, improve present products and operations, and be a leader in its industry.

WORKING CAPITAL

Working Capital is a very important number, particularly for those in management, who should follow this very carefully in managing their companies. It reflects the financial stability of the company and its ability to meet its present and future commitments of a financial nature. It is not always shown in the summaries, but it always appears in the Consolidated Statement of Changes in Financial Position, which shows the changes in working capital during the year. Working capital is one of the few important amounts that do not appear as a ratio but show the dollar amount of net working capital represented by total current assets less total current liabilities. Just move the decimal point over from the right to the left so that you just compare one or two digits appearing on the left side. If the total current assets is less than the current liabilities, there is a possible danger signal. Sometimes the ratio is expressed as 2 to 1, meaning that current assets are approximately $2 for each $1 of current liabilities. This may be stated in the management report as a current ratio of 2. Based upon a small sample, I find that the working capital ratio for industrial companies ranges from 1-1/2 to 3. Some major telephone companies and public utilities have a working capital ratio of less than 1. (AT&T is .89, Eastman Kodak is 2.5). This illustrates that each ratio must be related to the type of business and its working-capital needs.

Current assets represent cash or cash equivalents or other assets that will, in the normal course of business, be turned into cash within a twelve-month period or the company's normal business cycle. Current liabilities are those liabilities that have to be paid within the same period.

The working-capital ratio is generally more important to a creditor of the company than to the stockholder. Creditors want to be certain that they will be paid. On the other hand, stockholders are more anxious to be certain that the working capital is adequate for the continuing profitable operation of their company. A warning signal is when the ratio is lower and has been declining during several years without a reasonable explanation.

BOOK VALUE PER SHARE

"Book Value per Share" is usually stated in dollars and cents. It represents the equity referred to in the section on Return on Equity divided by the number of shares of common stock outstanding. Many profitable, well-run companies will have a book value per share less than the current market price. There are several reasons for this. The marketplace (the stock exchanges) evaluates the market price of a company by its present earning capacity and future potential. The book value per share is only an amount that is derived through the function of normal accounting under GAAP and does not represent the present value of the company as a going concern. The major concept is that assets are stated at cost less the appropriate amortization, depreciation, provisions for estimated losses, and so on.

If a company is forced into liquidation, the stockholders rarely recover book value. On the other hand, if there is a merger, buyout, or voluntary liquidation, stockholders may receive more than the book value per share.

"Book Value per Share" is a relationship that should be looked at and considered with all the other factors involved in your evaluation of the investment in the company. The book value per share will usually be found in the summary statements, and the growth of the company is often reflected in the increase in this number throughout the years.

DEBT TO EQUITY RATIO

The debt to equity ratio is used to determine the extent to which leverage is used by management in obtaining capital for its operations. By long-term debt, the company is able to increase the earnings for its common stockholders. On the other hand, if there is too much debt, the creditors may own more of the company than the stockholders do. Furthermore, a large debt may have an adverse impact upon earnings because of high interest rates. The ratio is rarely shown in the long-term operating summaries and is one that is easy to compute. Just look at the balance sheet and, if the amount of the long-term debt is as much as or more than the stockholders' equity, it will indicate that the lenders have invested more in the company than the stockholders. This might be a warning signal.

The other aspect is the number of times the company has earned its interest requirements. Interest expenses are generally shown as a separate item on the statement of earnings or the ten-year operating summary, and, if the net income before taxes on the same summary is an amount not too far removed from the interest expense, there is a danger signal. Failure to meet interest payments or repayment of the debt under the terms of the loan could cause problems. Look for information in the notes.

Management is fully aware of its problems with respect to excessive debt. Default on long-term debts is rare. It is not important to look into unless the company has had low earnings and low cash flow in recent years. This would indicate that its ability to meet its debt requirements may be in question.

MISCELLANEOUS RATIOS

There are a number of other ratios that might be considered. I will just mention them and what they disclose:

Depreciation to Fixed Assets

"Depreciation to Fixed Assets" is discussed in Chapter 11. This ratio discloses whether the plant is old, may need replacement, or could be inefficient.

Profit Margin

"Profit Margin," determined by dividing net income by sales, is useful for determining profit trends and comparing them with other companies' profit margins. If the margin increases, the company is operating efficiently and its product lines are improving. It appears frequently in five- or ten-year summaries.

Dividend Pay-out

Be dividing the total dollars of common-stock dividends paid by net income less preferred dividends (if any), you will arrive at the percentage of the net income paid to common-stock holders. If you are looking for high income from your investment, look for companies that have a high payout. If you want long-term growth and increased market value, invest in companies with a low payout, since they are reinvesting your earnings to improve the company without your having to pay any personal income tax on the retained earnings.

This list is far from complete. You can draw up some ratios yourself if you are so inclined. The more you explore the world of ratios the more you will learn about business, finance, analysis, and investing.

CONCLUSION

The use of ratios for security analysis is very important. You can spend as much or as little time as you feel appropriate for your particular circumstance. It is not the purpose of this book to go into a great deal about the technical aspects of the preparation and analysis of the annual report. This chapter is just to give you an overview. Appendix E will show you how some of the ratios are computed. If you want to know about them, go to the library, pick out books on ratio analysis that serve your purpose, and study them. Study them with pen, pencil, and a calculator or small computer. You will learn much about corporate finance, security analysis, and how to be a successful investor by using the same techniques that specialists use for the study and analysis of ratios.

14

A Case Study

INTRODUCTION

Some of the material in the previous chapters was pretty dull, uninteresting reading and sometimes difficult to understand. In order to give some life to the material previously discussed, I felt that a case study would be appropriate. However, with the hundreds of interesting annual reports that I have examined, it was difficult to select one that was appropriate. First, I thought that I would select a modest-sized, publicly owned company of say, $100 million in annual revenues. Several of these disclosed peculiarities that did not apply to the great mass of companies that are publicly owned. Then there was the problem of which industry to use. I finally decided to prepare a case study on a company of sufficient size to indicate that size was not the only criterion. The smaller companies were generally affected by outside circumstances so that the market value of the stock was not clearly reflected in the financial data reported in the annual report.

I hope that the folowing case study will help to clarify some of the subjects discussed in the earlier chapters.

THE COMPANY

What particularly attracted my interest in FMC Corporation was the cover of the annual report, which did not have the usual glossy picture but carried the following comment in bold letters:

> During the past year, FMC redirected substantial resources from low or average return businesses to those with higher returns. Through this selective process, FMC intends to achieve a fundamental improvement in its rate of return.

A brief description of the company on the inside of the cover is:

> As one of the world's leading producers of machinery and chemicals for industry, agriculture and government, FMC participates on a world-wide basis in selective segments of five broad markets: Industrial Chemicals, Petroleum Equipment and Services, Defense Equipment and Systems, Performance Chemicals and Specialized Machinery. FMC operates 129 manufacturing facilities and mines in 29 states and 14 foreign countries.

This company's products and markets encompass a broad scope of the economy to present enough problems and solutions for the investor to come to some conclusions reflecting the use of the procedures discussed in this book.

In order for you to follow the discussion hereinafter, I have included as Appendix C the significant pages of FMC's 1981 annual report. The pages that were read or scanned in the quick analysis of the 1981 annual report were:

	Page(s)
Financial summary	1
Letter from the Chairman of the Board and Chief Executive Officer	1–3
Review of operations by the President and Chief Operating Officer	4–7
Selective allocation of resources	8–9
Products and markets	20
Financial review	21–25
Consolidated financial statements	26–29
Notes to consolidated financial statements	30–36
Accountants' report	37
Management report on financial statements	37
10-year financial/operating summary	38–39

This is a good-sized company with sales from continuing operations of approximately $3.4 billion, net income from continuing operations of $176 million, total assets of $2.7 billion, and stockholders' equity of $1.3 billion. It has approximately 39,000 employees and 40,000 shareholders. Now let us see what we can find out from this rather attractive annual report by following the five major M's.

A QUICK REVIEW

The first thing that is evident upon a quick review of the letters from the chairman of the board and the president is their discussion of the anticipated increase of FMC's return on equity to 18 percent during the decade of the 1980s. This is a rather unusual approach and indicates management's candor in explaining to the stockholders in specific terms what they may expect and what the company's goals are. In addition, the president's letter includes the usual brief discussion of how well the company did and what progress it had made.

The next thing that caught my eye was two pages in which the chairman and the president discuss the strategy of selective allocation of resources and the implementation of the plan to reach the goal established. This is rather unusual when compared with other annual reports.

I next proceeded to scan the accountant's report and noticed that it consisted of the usual two paragraphs, standard report format. It did include as part of the last sentence the following: ". . . in conformity with generally accepted accounting principles which, except for the change in 1981 in the method of accounting for foreign currency translation as explained in Note 2 to the consolidated financial statements, have been applied on a consistent basis." This is a technical accounting change required by the FASB and therefore was not very significant except to professional analysts.

Next I looked at the management's report on financial statements, which again was the usual report and did not require any reading, other than a scan. I looked for unusual comments, of which there were none.

I then went to the ten-year financial summary on pages 38 and 39, which included a mass of data showing continuous growth from 1972 to 1981. Total revenue increased each year; net income increased each year except for 1976, 1980, and 1981. More about this later.

Primary earnings per share from continuing operations increased each year except for 1980, which was 2¢ less than 1979. I made a mental note to come back to this statement later and examine it a little more closely.

I then thumbed through the notice of annual meeting of stock-hlders and the proxy statement and found nothing unusual. I now proceed to the more intensive review of each of the big M's.

Management

All twelve members of the board of directors with one exception were up for reelection, and brief biographical sketches, including pictures, were included in the proxy statement. It looked like a good board with highly qualified individuals, including two officers of FMC, the chairman of the board, and the president. Of the remaining ten, all appeared to be outsiders. Paul L. Davies Jr., whose principal occupation is as partner in a major law firm, owned more than 17,000 shares to which could be added 6,500 shares owned by members of his family. All of the other board members owned fewer than 1,000 shares each.

Nothing is disclosed about any relationship between the law firm and the company. Although it is not stated in the annual report nor in the proxy statement, Mr. Davies is the son of one of the founders of the company. It may be thought that he is an insider, but this is not a very significant matter or it would have been disclosed in the proxy statement.

There is a good mixture of principal occupations and good age groups. The youngest is forty-seven, the oldest is sixty-five; one is in his forties, eight are in their fifties, and three are in their sixties.

Mr. Davies has been a director since 1965; all the others became directors in various years from 1970 to 1980. It would appear that this is a board consisting of independent, well-qualified individuals.

Committees. The board is organized into five standing committees of the usual classifications, including a Public Policy Committee, which reviews the company's governmental and legislative programs and relations, determines the appropriateness of the company's programs in such areas as affirmative action, environmental and product quality, employee safety and health, assesses the company's efforts to improve local employee community involvement, and reviews the activities of the company's charitable foundation. In other words, the company recognizes its obligations to the public.

Remuneration. The total remuneration to all directors and officers (a group of thirty-four individuals), consisting of salaries, bonuses, and fees, was $4,848,000, which is an average of $142,500 per individual. However, if we remove the two highest paid, the chairman of the board and the president, and the vice president, who receive an aggregate of $1,089,000, the others average $117,500 each, which appears to be fairly modest for a company of this size and complexity. The aggregate of the $4,848,000 represents about .15¢ per share which is less than 4% of total earnings.

It is rather difficult to evaluate these numbers just standing alone, so I decided that I would make a comparison with a company noted for its good management, Eastman Kodak Company. Eastman Kodak has a board of directors and officers' group of fifty-three who received $10,500,000 in remuneration, or an average of $198,000. For comparisons, Eastman Kodak sales were $10.3 billion and its earnings were $1.2 billion. Obviously it is larger than FMC. The two top officers received an aggregate of $1,380,000, and all others therefore received an average of $179,000. The aggregate officers' and directors' remuneration was 6.5¢ per share and represented approximately 8 percent of net income. It appears that although the numbers for FMC on the surface were high, they were not very much out of line when compared with those of one of the top companies in the United States.

The candor of the chairman of the board and the president in their respective letters to stockholders and the details disclosed in the annual report give confidence in the quality of the financial reporting and the information disclosed.

Earnings per Share Comparisons

Some concern could be expressed by looking at the five-year comparison on page thirty-seven of supplementary financial data adjusted for the effects of changing prices, which reports the market price per common share at year's end for each of the last five years. In the years 1977 through 1980, the stock closed at a low of $32.59 and a high of $33.82, but 1981 saw a decline to $25.63. This flat price range gives one concern about what the future might hold. Of course, 1981 was the year in which there was a bear market and many stocks were approaching a low at year end. Keep in mind that these market prices per common share at year end are adjusted for the effect of changing prices. In other words, they are adjusted for inflation. However, turning to page twenty-four, where we have quarterly financial information, we find that common-stock prices are reported for each quarter for 1980 and 1981, and this discloses the range for highs from the second quarter of 1980 of $24.88 to a high of $35.75 in the second quarter of 1981. The range for lows was from $21.63 in the first quarter of 1980 to $29.75 in the second quarter of 1981. It appears that the stock prices do not vary greatly during the year between high and low. This raises the question as to whether the market recognizes the potential of this company, if any. There appears to be a limited risk on the low side, but the potential on the high side probably depends upon a significant increase in the earnings per share if the plan to increase return on equity succeeds.

Based upon the above consideration, it appears that this company has a good, solid, conservative management. Apparently, it is beginning to take a more aggressive attitude toward increasing earnings and thereby improving the market price of its stock.

MONEY

The report of how management uses money for the benefit of stockholders, the company, and its officers and employees is reflected in the financial statements, in total. Let us see how the management of FMC manages its money.

On page one, the Financial Summary compares the current year, 1981, with 1980. To enable the reader to understand what is happening, the change, whether favorable or unfavorable, is reported in percentages. It looks pretty good. Even though total sales increased 5 percent, the income from continuing operations increased 25 percent and earnings per share 26 percent. On the other hand, the unfavorable variance for net income reflects the inclusion of the losses from discontinued operations. Dividends per share increased 10 percent, which may reflect the optimism of the board of directors that the results from continuing operations will continue to improve. So far, so good.

Consolidated Statements of Income

The official statement of income for the company, which was examined by the auditors and upon which they gave their opinion, is the Consolidated Statements of Income for the three years ended December 31, 1981, on page twenty-six.

The bottom lines show that net income and net income per share reflect a downward trend from 1979 through 1981. A quick examination indicates that this is principally from those operations that were discontinued during 1981. Income from continuing operations is pretty much a standoff for 1979 and 1980, but it improved considerably in 1981. This seems to indicate that the-decision made to restructure operations, which was first reported upon in the 1980 annual report, is successful. However, upon examining the details, we find that interest income increased by $18 million and other income increased by $10 million. Therefore, the increase in the income before income taxes of

$86 million resulted in part from $28 million nonoperating income and $58 million from operations.

Sales went up about $160 million. Cost of sales only went up $12 million. This is the real guts of what has happened as a result of restructuring, that is, an increase of $148 million. (Note how much easier it is to understand the numbers when we eliminate three digits from the right and discuss everything in millions of dollars.) This is not clear in the Statement of Income, so I made the following summary (slightly reclassified) in millions of dollars:

	1981	1980	Increase (decrease)
Sales	$3,367	$3,207	$160
Cost of sales	2,560	2,548	12
Gross profit from sales	807	659	148
Expenses	607	522	85
Operating income	200	137	63
Interest	41	23	18
Equity in earnings of affiliate	2	7	(5)
Other income	13	3	10
Income before income taxes	$ 256	$ 170	$ 86

Financial Review

The financial review on page twenty-two provides the answers to many questions that are raised or could be raised by someone analyzing the financial statements. One interesting aspect is the increase of approximately $738 million in the order backlog, principally in defense equipment and systems. Comparing segment sales for 1981, reported on page thirty-four, with the backlog data shows the following:

	1981 sales	Year-end backlog
	$ millions	
Petroleum equipment and services	$ 340	$ 210
Defense equipment and systems	582	2,020
Specialized machinery	1,086	491
	$2,008	$2,721

This comparison, on an overall basis, indicates that sales in 1982 may exceed those of 1981.

The analysis of working capital on page twenty-three shows a $50 million increase, reflecting a sound financial position that will give the company the financial wherewithal to implement its long-range plans.

Under capital expenditures, management points out where it is going to spend some of its money to increase volume and reduce costs. It is also interesting to note that most of the capital additions for 1981 of $272 million was paid for out of depreciation of $140 million plus $105 million from the sale of the Power Transmission Group (mentioned under working capital). This all appears to be well planned.

TEN-YEAR FINANCIAL OPERATING SUMMARY

Although an examination of the consolidated statements of income is helpful, the most interesting financial statement from the stockholder's viewpoint is the ten-year financial operating summary on page thirty-eight. I have already touched on some of this in our analysis under the section on management.

The dividends per common share have doubled in a ten-year period as a result of modest increases each year. This shows a very conservative approach. Management evidently feels that it is in the best interest of stockholders to reinvest some of the earnings for future growth. It appears that the basic philosophy of the management is to declare dividends of approximately 40 percent of the earnings per share. If the income is increased to 18 percent of the stockholders' equity, it can be considered that there could be significant increases in the dividends paid.

The earnings per share for 1981 were significantly reduced as a result of the loss from discontinued operations of $1.13 per share. However, this was a one-shot deal, and it can be readily perceived that 1982 earnings should be significantly higher than the $3.87 reported for 1981.

Another interesting line on this report is net income as a percentage of average stockholders' equity. The high point was 14.1 percent in 1978. The low point was 7.6 percent in 1972. It has been averaging around 11 percent for most of the years. The 18 percent goal is rather an ambitious program based upon experience, and it might take several years before it can be reached. Looking at this chart, we can see that if the company can increase income as a percent of average stockholders' equity by one percentage point each year, it will reach its objective in seven years.

Another interesting line is income from continuing operations before extraordinary items as a percentage of sales. The high point that had been attained in 1973, 1976, and 1977 has been 5.8 percent. Nineteen-eighty-one was 5.2 percent, which showed a .8 percent increase from 1980. If the 5.8 percent can be reached in 1982, we will begin to see quite a turnaround in this company.

The labor force based on employees at year's end has been at a plateau since 1977. The peak of 40,984 was reached in 1979 and is now down to 38,940. With increased labor costs, a reduction of the labor force can contribute measurably to the success of the company's plans.

There are many other conclusions that could be reached by more detailed analysis of these ten-year financial statements, but those that I've discussed are the ones that I think will have the greatest impact upon the future.

INFLATION

The study of such a long-range period raises the question about the impact of inflation. This is discussed in Note 18: supplementary information on the effects of changes in prices, starting on page thirty-five, which compares the years 1979 through 1981 adjusted for changing prices. As an academic exercise, it appears that the company is about holding its own. If it can continue to increase its income and continue to increase the dividends payable to stockholders plus the increase that will arise out of the 18 percent goal, at the end of the 1980s the stockholders will have gained more than they would have lost through inflation.

There are three columns in the statement on page thirty-six showing (1) the significant items as reported in the primary financial statements, (2) adjustment for general inflation, which is generally referred to as "constant dollars," and (3) adjustment for changes in specific prices, generally referred to as "current cost." These are explained in some detail and might be interesting to study.

We note that there is relatively little change between cost of sales as reported and cost of sales adjusted for inflation. The principal reason is that the LIFO (last-in, first-out) method is used for pricing inventories for financial purposes, which eliminates the effect of inflation in costs. LIFO requires that the most recent purchases, which would usually be at higher prices, be charged against current costs as the inventory is consumed or sold.

The big change is in the provision for depreciation. In the primary financial statements, depreciation expense is based upon original historical cost. In the other statements, it is based upon replacement cost either for constant dollars or for current cost. This clearly points up what is often said: that the depreciable assets are generally under valued on balance sheets and therefore the company is not earning enough money at historical costs to replace the wear and tear and the obsolescence of the equipment. However, when you consider that all major companies have had this problem in varying degrees throughout their entire existence and that they have survived and even grown, you can see that management provided for this by building up of reserves through retained earnings. Furthermore, as frequently is the case, old machinery and equipment is replaced and the newer replacement costs more than the old—but it also is more efficient. Sometimes this increased efficiency more than offsets the inflationary cost.

NOTES TO THE CONSOLIDATED FINANCIAL STATEMENTS

Time could be spent and wasted in reading all the details in the Notes to the Consolidated Financial Statements. These notes range from highly technical subjects required by the FASB and the SEC—of interest only to the professional—to interesting comments that have a direct bearing on understanding the financial statements. They include details for some of the numbers included in the statement. An investor can be selective and still learn a lot. Let us see how we can choose and still improve our knowledge about FMC.

Notes begin on page thirty. It might be advisable to read Note 1 in its entirety if it is the first time that you are examining the financial statements of a company. This note usually pertains to principal accounting policies. I did not study it in detail since I had examined FMC for the past three years. Generally, this note is the same as in previous years. If there is any major change, it will be highlighted in the auditor's opinion.

"Inventories" is one of the items that I looked at to see if there was any change between FIFO and LIFO.

Although the auditor's opinion refers to Note 2 about foreign currency translation, I didn't bother reading it since this is technical change.

Note 3 describes the major divestitures and acquisitions, and, in this case, it gives the information you require in order to understand and evaluate discontinued operations. It explains what was disposed and how much was obtained. It also describes how the accounting was handled and the effect upon earnings.

Another note of interest is Note 5—Inventories. This explains that the current replacement cost exceeded inventories recorded at LIFO at December 31, 1981, by $366 million. This means that current assets would be $366 million more if the inventories were at the lower of cost or market, the usual FIFO treatment. Furthermore, it would increase working capital and total assets by the same amount. In other words, there is a hidden profit in the inventory. What occurred when FMC first went on LIFO some years back was an adjustment reducing the then–existing inventory to the LIFO basis. That was in 1974. For each year, as the inventory grew, there was a minor effect upon the earnings. Earnings would have been a little higher than reported. If inventories were reduced, the liquidation of the low-cost inventory would reflect as higher profits in that year's reported income. What I am saying here is that using the LIFO method is a conservative way of accounting and reporting. The usual purpose of LIFO inventory is to reduce taxes, which it does effectively. But the Internal Revenue Code says that if you use LIFO for tax purposes, you must use it for financial-statement reporting purposes. This then became a generally accepted accounting principle. Furthermore, LIFO reduces the adverse effect of inflation.

The next note that was examined was Number 8, Property, Plant and Equipment. The accumulated depreciation was compared with property, plant, and equipment at historical cost. In this instance, accumulated depreciation was approximately 40 percent of historical cost, which is about par for the course. If the accumulated depreciation approaches 50 percent or more, there may be a problem in that the fixed assets are growing older and therefore may not be as efficient as they could be, or that they have to be replaced soon, requiring the use of substantial funds that might impair working capital.

As previously stated, it appears that the company has been following a sound management approach for capital additions using retained earnings and the proceeds from the sale of discontinued plant. This is discussed in the Financial Review (page twenty-two) under 'Liquidity and Capital Resources." It is also reflected in the Consolidated Statement of Changes in Financial Position, where Provision for Depreciation, the proceeds from the sale of discontinued operations, and other property and plant is shown as a source of working capital. Working capital is a very important amount that isn't highlighted to a great degree in most reports. The increase or decrease is always shown in the Consolidated Statement of Changes in Financial Position. In the case of FMC, the amount of working capital is reported in the ten-year Summary (page thirty). It shows a fairly stable position from 1976 to the present.

Let's get back to the notes. FMC Finance Corporation is not included in the consolidated figures in its entirety and therefore is shown separately in Note 7. However, the stockholders' equity as shown on the balance sheet and the increase or decrease for the year is shown as Equity in Earnings of Affiliates in the statement of earnings so that, on an overall basis, it is included in the retained earnings, in the total assets, and in stockholders' equity.

Note 10 describes long-term debts in detail. That portion that becomes due within the next twelve months is shown under current liabilities. It also shows how much of the long-term debt will become due within the following four years. This will enable the reader of the report to determine what drain there might be upon working capital to meet these long-term debts. Given the size of this company, the size of its earnings, and the flow of working capital, it should have no difficulty in meeting the requirements of the various long-term debts. It is also interesting to note that the interest rates are reasonable and that approximately $73 million long-term is convertible into common stock, although this note does not indicate the rate. That is reported in Note 12—Stockholders' Equity.

The next note (No. 11) pertains to income taxes. This is a subject that requires close attention, and it appears that the company has been administering its taxes fairly well. Although the expected United States tax rate is 46 percent, it has been paying taxes at an effective rate of 31 percent in 1981 and 18 percent in 1980. The biggest changes are due to investment credit (tax benefits from purchasing machinery and equipment), percentage depletion (tax benefits from using natural resources obtained by mining operations), and foreign earnings subject to lower taxes. Also, it is interesting to note that the years through 1973 have been examined by the U.S. Treasury and have been settled.

In Note 12, Stockholders' Equity, the amount of the stockholders' equity available for distribution to stockholders as dividends was reported as $1,118 million retained earnings, only $172 million of which was restricted. Therefore, the impact upon shareholders is minor.

It also discusses the convertible features and the conversion amounts. Since the redemption rates of the preferred stock is $50 per share and each share is convertible into 1¼ shares of common stock, the market price of the common stock must be in excess of $40 per share before conversion is advisable. With $41.50 conversion rate for the 4¼ percent debentures, the possibility of conversion is not currently effective. On the other hand, the 4⅞ percent convertible debentures are convertible at $31.10 per a share of common stock, which is less than the market prices during recent periods; it appears that, as this is written, the conversion may be feasible at any time.

Note 13, Segment Information, is of interest. The significant matter is to examine the various segments of the business to see whether these are businesses that you want to invest in. If the answer is yes, then to what extent do these segments contribute to the earnings of FMC? With your usual judgment, decide what you think the company should do with respect to those segments (see discussion of SEC regulation S-K Chapter 3 and Chapter 12) and how this affects your judgment on the company's stock. In the same footnote on page thirty-five, there is a schedule of operations by geographic areas. A company such as FMC is operating all over the world, and again, this is a question of judgment as to whether you want to be involved with a company that has 90 percent of its business in the United States and 10 percent elsewhere with all the risks involved in foreign operations. It appears, however, that these operations, particularly those in Western Europe, are rather successful, contributing 10 percent of the company's sales and income before taxes.

Note 16 gives the story on lease commitments. Leases are, in effect, long-term commitments, and it is worthwhile to examine this note to see whether leases are reasonable considering the size of the company. A quick look at the amounts for operating leases in relation to the size of FMC reveals that they appear nominal.

Note 17 pertains to Contingent Liabilities. Apparently there are no material contingent liabilities. This is a note that should be examined carefully in any report because contingent liabilities, if they no longer are contingent, may become active major liabilities and could be a disaster.

Note 18 pertains to the effect of inflation and should be examined. It was explained previously under the "Inflation" caption. Don't become too concerned about this subject; the effect on FMC was not significant.

So much for the notes. If they are read with good judgment, much can be learned about the company and its management. The above comments are a partial indication of one man's views from a quick reading without studying each note in depth.

MATERIALS AND MERCHANDISE (INVENTORIES)

Inventories represent materials available to be made into merchandise and products for sale, materials and products that are ready for sale, and useable items that are to be charged against cost in various ways. It is usually a significant item on the balance sheet as a part of working capital, and FMC is no exception with total inventories of $484 million as of December 1981. The reference to Note 5 on inventories indicates that FMC's inventory is reported on the LIFO basis, and the statement is made that "The current replacement cost of inventories exceeded the lower of LIFO cost or market carrying values by approximately $366 million." In other words, if these inventories were reported at current cost, it would be about $850 million.

There is approximately $410 million of "inventoried costs," at cost, or realizable value relating to long-term contracts and programs included in this inventory. This is work-in-progress for long-term contracts determined upon the costs incurred or realizable value, depending upon which is the lower. Many of these projects are under contracts that provide for progress payments. There have been $284 million of progress payments deducted from the cost value of the inventories on hand at December 31, 1981, so from a balance sheet viewpoint, the company is in a sound position with respect to these transactions.

A simple association between inventories and cost of sales indicates that the inventory is one-fifth of the cost of sales of approximately $2,500 million. This means that there is a turnover of this inventory value of about five times in a year, which is a good operating number and a good statistic. It appears that management is cognizant of its inventory problems and situations and is in a sound position.

MACHINERY, PLANT, AND EQUIPMENT

As previously mentioned, Note 8 describes the investment in property, plant, and equipment for 1980 and 1981. The net value of approximately $1,200 million is after deducting $820 million of accumulated depreciation applicable to total costs of $2,020 million. This appears to be a satisfactory ratio in that the machinery and equipment are depreciated only about 40 percent. It also implies that the machinery and equipment are fairly modern. The accounting principles involved for recording property, plant, and equipment as stated in Note 1 is that depreciation is charged principally on a straight-line basis using lives that approximate those permitted by the 1962 Internal Revenue Service guideline regulations. It appears that these rates are reasonable. It also states that maintenance and repairs are charged to expense in the years incurred.

The Consolidated Statement of Changes in Financial Position disclosed that there were capital expenditures in 1981 of $272 million, which, of course, had to be paid from current working capital resulting principally from two sources: (1) provision for depreciation included in the normal income operations of $140 million and (2) proceeds from sale of discontinued operations of $110 million and disposal of property, plant, and equipment of $28 million. This totals $278 million, which exceeds capital expenditures by $6 million. It is evident that the conservative management of this company tries to maintain the working-capital position without converting current assets into fixed assets.

MARKETS

On page twenty, the company lists products and markets by industry segments, operating units, and principal products and services. It shows most major industries, consumer goods, to agricultural, pharmaceuticals, construction, utilities, United States and foreign national governments and many others. It would appear that they are not dependent to any great extent on any one source of business. For example, $582 million in sales of defense equipment and systems, which probably are the major sales to governments, represents a little more than 15 percent of the total sales. Another 15 percent of the sales is in international operations, principally Latin America, Canada, and Western Europe. Only $37 million went to Asia, Africa, and other places that could be problem areas and represents only 1 percent of the total sales.

Accordingly, the company's marketing program is well balanced so that a major problem in any one area would not have a serious effect upon the company.

CONCLUSION

It appears that this is a well-managed, conservatively operated, successful business. There has been growth; it has been slow but at a steady and reasonable rate. There should be more of the same for the future. Moreover, the present management as represented by the board of directors and the present officers has embarked upon a long-range program to enhance its growth and profitability. It is too soon to evaluate the potential for its success. Given its history, however, it is reasonable to assume that the company's earnings will grow at the rate of approximately 10 percent per year, that dividends will increase by the same percent, and that there is the possibility that this will be reflected in the market price of the stock.

A comparison of the high and low of each of the years shows a spread of about $10 a share and a slow increment. This is not a very glamorous stock as far as the stock market is concerned, but this is a good, solid company, and, depending upon such outside influences on the market price as the general movement of the Dow Jones Industrial averages, the effects of inflation, the economic climate, and the many other intangibles that affect stock market prices, the market price for this stock should rise slowly. Between dividends and increments to the market value of the stock, it can result in a fairly successful investment over a long-range period.

Keep in mind that only a few selected matters were discussed in this chapter. For someone who wants to go to greater depth, there are many more ratios and interesting comparisons that can be made, but this chapter can give you a good idea of what can be learned in a reasonable period of time in the analysis of a fairly complex company.

1982 ANNUAL REPORT

Nineteen-eighty-two was a year of business recession that affected most corporate enterprises. FMC was no exception. The effect was spelled out in the first sentence of the letter of the chairman of the board, which says, "Although sales increased 4% over the 1981 level, income from continuing operations and primary earnings per share each declined 14%." Later on in this letter he states, "Unquestionably, the recession which took hold in 1981 and deepened throughout 1982 has impeded the company's short-term progress towards its objective of higher financial returns. However, we remain committed to the achievement of our primary goal of an 18% return on equity during the decade." Turning to the ten-year financial operating summary, we find that the data reported confirm this, showing a per share reduction in earnings of 65¢ per share to $4.23. In its goal toward the return on equity of 18 percent, the company has moved up slightly from 11 percent to 11.5 percent. Most of the other statistics are quite comparable with those of the prior year.

Similarly, the market prices of the common stock are comparable with those of 1981. The 1982 range of quarterly highs was from 27⅝ to 35 as compared with 1981 of 27⅞ to 35¾. The low range was from 23⅛ to 29 compared with 24¼ to 29¾. It appears that the company is holding its own in its plans for improvement and that nothing materially has changed except the desire of the company to reach certain goals. This is described very clearly in the headline on the front cover, which shows some bar charts comparing 1979 with 1982 Research and Development expenditures and states boldly, "By concentrating research and development expenditures in high-return businesses, FMC intends to strengthen its portfolio and raise long-term returns."

It appears that our opinion of this company has not changed by any information available since we analyzed the 1981 annual report in early 1982.

ADDENDA

The analysis of the 1981 annual report and my conclusion which makes up the major portion of this chapter was written during the spring of 1982. The brief survey of the 1982 annual report was completed in the spring of 1983. It is now March 20, 1984. The 1983 annual report has not yet been published. From news releases, it would appear that FMC is doing well. At least, its stock has been performing well on the stock exchange. In spite of declining stock prices as evidenced by the Dow Jones Industrial Average (the most important index followed by investors), FMC closed on March 19 at 42½. The twelve months high and low were 48¾ and 35, compared with 1981 high and low of 35¾ and 24¼. It would appear the program is a success.

Appendixes

APPENDIX A: DEFINITIONS OF ABBREVIATIONS

AIA	American Institute of Accountants
AICPA	American Institute of Certified Public Accountants
APB	Accountants Principles Board
ARB	Accounting Research Bulletins
ASR	Accounting Series Releases (SEC)
CPA	Certified public accountant (as used in this book, usually a professional independent certified public accountant)
FASB	Financial Accounting Standards Board
FIFO	First in, first out (inventory method)
Form 10-K	Annual Report required to be filed with the SEC
GAAP	Generally accepted accounting principles
GAAS	Generally accepted auditing standards
IRS	Internal Revenue Service
LIFO	Last in, first out (inventory method)
NYSE	New York Stock Exchange
P/E	Price/earnings ratio
POB	Public Oversight Board

SAP	Statements on Auditing Procedure
SAS	Statements on Auditing Standards
SEC	Securities and Exchange Commission
S-K	A regulation amending regulation S-X
S-X	A regulation describing form and content for financial statements

APPENDIX B: EXCERPT FROM 1980 ANNUAL REPORT

Accountants' Report

To the Shareholders and Directors
of Johns-Manville Corporation:

We have examined the consolidated balance sheets of Johns-Manville Corporation as of December 31, 1980 and 1979, and the related consolidated statements of earnings and earnings reinvested and changes in financial position for each of the three years in the period ended December 31, 1980. Our examinations were made in accordance with generally accepted auditing standards and, accordingly, included such tests of the accounting records and such other auditing procedures as we considered necessary in the circumstances. The financial statements of Canadian subsidiaries, which reflect total assets constituting 10% in 1980 and 1979, and net sales constituting 10%, 9% and 11% in 1980, 1979 and 1978, respectively, of the related consolidated totals were examined by other auditors whose report thereon has been furnished to us. Our opinion expressed herein, insofar as it relates to amounts included for Canadian subsidiaries examined by other auditors, is based solely upon their report.

As discussed in Note 5 to the consolidated financial statements, the Company is a defendant in a substantial and increased number of asbestos/health legal actions.[1] *The ultimate liability resulting from these matters cannot presently be reasonably estimated. In our report* dated February 1, 1980, our opinion on the Company's consolidated financial position as of December 31, 1979 was unqualified. However, because of the increased uncertainties that developed during 1980 with respect to these matters, our present opinion on the consolidated financial position as of December 31, 1979, as presented herein, is different from that expressed in our previous report.

In our opinion, based upon our examinations and the report of other auditors, the aforementioned financial statements present fairly the consolidated results of operations and changes in financial position of Johns-Manville Corporation for each of the three years in the period ended December 31, 1980 and, *subject to the effects of adjustments that might have been required had the outcome of the uncertainties referred to in the preceding paragraph been known,* the consolidated financial position of Johns-Manville Corporation at December 31, 1980 and 1979, in conformity with generally accepted accounting principles applied on a consistent basis.

Coopers & Lybrand
February 4, 1981
Denver, Colorado

---

[1]Italics not in original.

Note 5—Contingencies

The Company is a defendant or co-defendant in a substantial number of lawsuits brought by present or former insulation workers, shipyard workers, factory workers and other persons alleging damage to their health from exposure to dust from asbestos fiber or asbestos-containing products manufactured or sold by the Company and, in most cases, by certain other defendants. The majority of these claims allege that the Company and other defendants failed in their duty to warn of the hazards of inhalation of asbestos fiber and dust originating from asbestos-containing products. In the opinion of Management, the Company has substantial defenses to these legal actions, resulting in part from prompt warnings of the possible hazards of exposure to asbestos fiber emitted from asbestos-containing insulation products following the 1964 publication of scientific studies linking pulmonary disease in insulation workers to asbestos exposure.

Also included in these legal actions are a number of cases brought by some of the company's own employees and by employees of other manufacturing companies which use asbestos fiber in their operations. These suits typically allege that the Company and other defendants failed to warn of the hazards associated with the use of such fiber. In the opinion of Management, the Company has substantial defenses to these legal actions including the fact that, with respect to employees of other manufacturing companies, it had no special knowledge not in the possession of the plaintiffs' employers which would give rise to a special duty on the part of the Company, and, with respect to the employees of the Company, that applicable workers' compensation statutes provide appropriate defenses to most such claims.

It is the Company's belief that the claims and lawsuits pending and which may arise in the future relate to events and conditions existing in prior years. More specifically, it is the Company's belief, based on the following factors and assumptions, that since at least prior to the period covered by these financial statements, no significant new potential liabilities have been created for the Company with respect to diseases known to be related to asbestos and arising from asbestos fiber and/or asbestos-containing products manufactured or sold by the Company:

- That since the mid-1970's, the Company has sold asbestos fiber in the United States only in pressure pack, block form or other similar condition and not in a loose form;
- That by 1973, the Company had ceased domestic manufacture of thermal insulation products containing asbestos which are the products principally involved in disease claims made against the Company;
- That the Occupational Safety and Health Administration (OSHA) established a maximum exposure standard for asbestos fiber of five fibers per cubic centimeter in 1972 and lowered that standard to two fibers per cubic centimeter in 1976. It is assumed that compliance with such standards in the work place was achieved within a reasonable time following such promulgation and is continuing to date; and
- With respect to any use not complying with the OSHA asbestos standards, the Company's defensive posture with respect to claims arising out of such environments will be significantly enhanced.

As of December 31, 1980, the Company was a defendant or co-defendant in 5,087 asbestos/health suits brought by approximately 9,300 individual plaintiffs. This represents a substantial increase from the December 31, 1979 level of 2,707 cases (brought by approximately 4,100 plaintiffs) and the December 31, 1978 level of 1,181 cases (brought by approximately 1,500 plaintiffs). During 1979, the Company was named as a defendant in an average of 141 cases per month (brought by an average of 196 plaintiffs) as compared with an average of 65 cases per month (brought by an average of 83 plaintiffs) in 1978. During the first three quarters of 1980, the Company was named as a defendant in an average of 194 cases per month (brought by an average of 382 plaintiffs); this rate inceased to an average of 304 cases per month (brought by an average of 403 plaintiffs) in the fourth quarter of 1980. During 1980 the Company disposed of 402 claims at an average disposition cost (excluding legal expenses) of $23,300, substantially all of which was paid by applicable insurance. This level of disposition cost represents a significant growth from the pre-1980 level of approximately $13,000 per claim. The growth in these two areas has significantly increased the uncertainties as to the future number of similar claims which the Company may receive, and the future disposition costs of the pending and future claims. Also during 1980, to resolve uncertainties as to the correct interpretation of a number of provisions in the various policies of insurance maintained by the Company and applicable to these claims, it was necessary for the Company to bring a declaratory judgment action to have such issues resolved by a court of law. While it continues to be the Company's opinion that its position with

respect to these issues is sound and in accord with the weight of judicial precedents, any litigation involves uncertainties to some degree.

Because of the uncertainties associated with the asbestos/health litigation, and in spite of the substantial defenses the Company believes it has with respect to these claims, the eventual outcome of the asbestos/health litigation cannot be predicted at this time and the ultimate liability of the Company after application of available insurance cannot be estimated with any degree of reliability. No reasonable estimate of loss can be made and no liability has been recorded in the financial statements. Liabilities, if any, relating to asbestos/health litigation will be recorded in accordance with generally accepted accounting principles when such amounts can be reasonably estimated. Depending on how and when these uncertainties are resolved, the cost to the Company could be substantial.

APPENDIX C: EXCERPT FROM 1981 ANNUAL REPORT

Accountants' Report

To the Shareholders and Directors
of Manville Corporation:

We have examined the consolidated balance sheets of Manville Corporation as of December 31, 1981 and 1980, and the related consolidated statements of earnings and earnings reinvested and changes in financial position for each of the three years in the period ended December 31, 1981. Our examinations were made in accordance with generally accepted auditing standards and, accordingly, included such tests of the accounting records and such other auditing procedures as we considered necessary in the circumstances. The financial statements of Canadian subsidiaries, which reflect total assets and net sales constituting approximately 10% of the related consolidated totals, were examined by other auditors whose report thereon has been

furnished to us. Our opinion expressed herein, insofar as it relates to amounts included for Canadian subsidiaries examined by other auditors, is based solely upon their report.

As discussed in Note 5 to the consolidated financial statements, Johns-Manville Corporation (a wholly-owned subsidiary of Manville Corporation) is a defendant in a substantial number of asbestos-health legal actions.[1] *The ultimate liability resulting from these matters cannot presently be reasonably estimated.*

In our opinion, based upon our examinations and the report of other auditors, the aforementioned financial statements present fairly the consolidated results of operations and changes in financial position of Manville Corporation for

---

[1]Italics not in original.

each of the three years in the period ended December 31, 1981 and, *subject to the effects of adjustments that might have been required had the outcome of the uncertainties referred to in the preceding paragraph been known, the consolidated financial position of Manville Corporation at December 31, 1981 and 1980, in* *conformity with generally accepted accounting principles applied on a consistent basis.*

Coopers & Lybrand
February 5, 1982
Denver, Colorado

Note 5—Contingencies

Johns-Manville Corporation and certain of its subsidiaries ("J-M" or "Johns-Manville") is a defendant or co-defendant in a substantial number of lawsuits brought by present or former insulation workers, shipyard workers, factory workers and other persons alleging damage to their health from exposure to dust from asbestos fibers or asbestos-containing products manufactured or sold by J-M and, in most cases, by certain other defendants. The majority of these claims allege J-M and other defendants failed in their duty to warn of the hazards of inhalation of asbestos fiber and dust originating from asbestos-containing products. J-M believes it has substantial defenses to these legal actions, resulting in part from prompt warnings of the possible hazards of exposure to asbestos fiber emitted from asbestos-containing insulation products following the 1964 publication of scientific studies linking pulmonary disease in insulation workers to asbestos exposure.

Also included in these legal actions are a number of cases brought by some employees of J-M and certain of its subsidiaries and by employees of other manufacturing companies which used asbestos fiber in their operations. These suits typically allege that J-M, its subsidiaries, and other defendants failed to warn of the hazards associated with the use of such fiber. J-M believes it has substantial defenses to these legal actions including the fact that, with respect to employees of other manufacturing companies, it had no special knowledge not in the possession of the plaintiffs' employers which would give rise to a special duty on the part of J-M, and, with respect to the employees of J-M subsidiaries, that applicable workers' compensation statutes provide appropriate defenses to many aspects of such claims and there are substantial defenses to other aspects of such claims.

J-M believes that the claims and lawsuits pending and which may arise in the future relate to events and conditions existing in prior years. More specifically, it is J-M's belief, based on the following factors and assumptions, that since at least the beginning of 1978, no significant new potential liabilities have been created for J-M with respect to diseases known to be related to asbestos and arising from asbestos fiber and/or asbestos-containing products manufactured or sold by J-M:

• That since the mid-1970's, J-M has sold asbestos fiber in the United States only in pressure pack, block form or other similar condition and not in a loose form;

• That by 1973, J-M had ceased domestic manufacture of thermal insulation products containing asbestos which are the products principally involved in disease claims made against J-M;

• That the Occupational Safety and Health Administration (OSHA) established a maximum exposure standard for asbestos fiber of five fibers per cubic centimeter in 1972 and lowered that standard to two fibers per cubic centimeter in 1976. It is assumed that compliance with such standards in the work place was achieved within a reasonable time following such promulgation and is continuing to date; and

• With respect to any use not complying with the OSHA asbestos standards., J-M's defensive posture with respect to claims arising out of such environments will be significantly enhanced.

As of December 31, 1981, J-M was a defendant or co-defendant in approximately 9,300 asbestos-health suits brought by approximately

12,800 individual plaintiffs. This represents an increase over the December 31, 1980 level of 5,087 cases (brought by approximately 9,300 plaintiffs) and a substantial increase over the December 31, 1979 level of 2,707 cases (brought by approximately 4,100 plaintiffs) and the December 31, 1978 level of 1,181 cases (brought by approximately 1,500 plaintiffs). During 1979, J-M was named as a defendant in an average of 141 cases per month (brought by an average of 196 plaintiffs) as compared with an average of 65 cases per month (brought by an average of 83 plaintiffs) in 1978. During the first three quarters of 1980, J-M was named as a defendant in an average of 194 cases per month (brought by an average of 382 plaintiffs); this rate increased to an average of 304 cases per month (brought by an average of 403 plaintiffs) in the fourth quarter of 1980 and to an average of 400 cases per month (brought by an average of 525 plaintiffs) during 1981. During 1980, J-M disposed of 401 claims at an average disposition cost of $22,600, and during 1981, a total of 802 claims were disposed of, with J-M's share of disposition costs being an average of $15,430 per claim. All disposition cost references exclude legal expenses, and the verdicts in approximately 20 cases which are presently on appeal (where the average judgment against J-M is approximately $223,360). Substantially all of these disposition costs have been charged to applicable insurance. The 1980 and 1981 level of disposition costs represents a significant growth from the pre-1980 level of approximately $13,000 per claim and results in an increase in the overall disposition cost per plaintiff through December 31, 1981 to approximately $15,640. The growth in these two areas (volume and costs) has significantly increased the uncertainties as to the future number of similar claims which J-M may receive, and the future disposition costs of the pending and future claims. During 1980, to resolve uncertainties as to the correct interpretation of a number of provisions in the various policies of insurance maintained by J-M and applicable to these claims, it was necessary for J-M to bring a declaratory judgment action to have such issues resolved by a court of law. While it continues to be J-M's opinion that its position with respect to these issues is sound and in accord with the weight of judicial precedent, any litigation involves uncertainties to some degree.

Because of the uncertainties associated with the asbestos-health litigation, and in spite of the substantial defenses J-M believes it has with respect to these claims, the eventual outcome of the asbestos-health litigation cannot be predicted at this time and the ultimate liability of J-M after application of available insurance cannot be reasonably determined in accordance with Financial Accounting Standards Board Statement No. 5, "Accounting for Contingencies". No reasonable determination of loss can be made and no liability has been recorded in the financial statements. Liabilities relating to asbestos-health litigation will be recorded in accordance with generally accepted accounting principles when such amounts can be determined. *Depending on how and when these uncertainties with respect to J-M are resolved, the cost to J-M and thus to Manville Corporation could be substantial.*

Costs associated with asbestos-health claims are presented separately in the 1981 financial statements because of the increased activity related to such claims. The 1980 financial statements, which have not been reclassified to conform to the 1981 presentation, include approximately $8.5 million of similar costs that is reflected in cost of sales and selling, general and administrative expenses. Amounts relating to 1979 were not material.

APPENDIX D: EXCERPT FROM 1982 ANNUAL REPORT

Accountants' Report

To the Shareholders and Directors of
  MANVILLE CORPORATION:

We have examined the consolidated balance sheets of Manville Corporation as of December 31, 1982 and 1981, and the related consolidated statements of operations and earnings reinvested and changes in financial position for each of the three years in the period ended December 31, 1982. Our examinations were made in accordance with generally accepted auditing standards and, accordingly, included such tests of the accounting records and such other auditing procedures as we considered necessary in the circumstances. The financial statements of Canadian subsidiaries, which reflect total assets and net sales ranging from 6% to 10% of the related consolidated totals, were examined by other auditors whose reports thereon have been furnished to us. Our opinion expressed herein, insofar as it relates to amounts included for Canadian subsidiaries examined by other auditors, is based solely upon their reports.

As discussed in Note 1 to the consolidated financial statements, Johns-Manville Corporation (a wholly-owned subsidiary of Manville Corporation) is a defendant in a substantial number of asbestos-health legal actions.[1] *On August 26, 1982, Manville Corporation and substantially all of its United States and Canadian subsidiaries filed separate petitions for reorganization under Chapter 11 of the Bankruptcy Reform Act of 1978, as amended, because of contingent liabilities resulting from pending and potential litigation related to the asbestos-health issue. The ultimate liability resulting from these matters cannot presently be reasonable estimated.*

In our opinion, based upon our examinations and the reports of other auditors, the financial statements referred to above present fairly the consolidated results of operations and changes in financial position of Manville Corporation for each of the three years in the period ended December 31, 1982 and, *subject to the effects of adjustments that might have been required had the outcome of the uncertainties referred to in the preceding paragraph been known, the consolidated financial position of Manville Corporation at December 31, 1982 and 1981, in conformity with generally accepted accounting principles applied on a consistent basis.*

Coopers & Lybrand
February 22, 1983
Denver, Colorado

Manville Corporation
Notes to Consolidated Financial Statements

Note 1—Chapter 11 Proceedings

On August 26, 1982, Manville Corporation and substantially all of its United States and Canadian consolidated subsidiaries (the "Debtor Corporations") filed separate petitions in the United States Bankruptcy Court for the Southern District of New York (the "Bankruptcy Court") seeking reorganization under Chapter 11 of the Bankruptcy Reform Act of 1978, as amended (the "Bankruptcy Code"). The filings were precipitated by contingent liabilities resulting from pending and potential litigation related to the asbestos-health issue. See the discussion provided in ITEM 3. LEGAL PROCEEDINGS, regarding the pending Chapter 11 proceedings.

Under Chapter 11, substantially all litigation and claims against the Debtor Corporations at the date of the filings have been stayed while the Debtor Corporations continue business operations as debtors-in-possession. Interest on unsecured obligations of the Debtor Corporations has not been accrued in the consolidated financial statements since the date of the filing of the petitions for reorganization. In addition, no dividend has been declared or accrued on the Company's cumulative preferred or common stock since that date.

On August 26, 1982, litigation was pending on behalf of approximately 16,500 persons seeking damages for injuries alleged to have resulted from exposure to asbestos fiber or asbestos-containing products manufactured or sold by one or more of the Debtor Corporations. On the basis of epidemiological and statistical reports, using conservative assumptions favorable to Manville, Manville Corporation projected that more than 32,000 additional asbestos-health related lawsuits would be filed against one or more of the Debtor Corporations by the year 2001.

[1]Italics not in original.

Those reports also resulted in the conclusion that the Company's disposition costs for the asbestos-health related claims, whether or not currently asserted (the "A-H Claims"), if they continued to be resolved through conventional tort litigation, would average at least $40,000 per claim. The $40,000 per claim projection was estimated in the reports through the use of statistical smoothing techniques applied to the Company's recent disposition cost excluding punitive damages (as opposed to historical averages). Included in this $40,000 amount is approximately $7,500 per claim for Manville's outside legal expenses. If the disposition cost (including legal fees) of the A-H Claims were to average approximately $40,000 per claim as projected, the aggregate cost of disposing of the A-H Claims through conventional tort litigation would be at least $1.9 billion. The Company's historical average disposition cost for all cases disposed of through December 31, 1982 (approximately 4,110 claims) is $16,845 per claim excluding legal costs and verdicts on appeal.

There is substantial uncertainty whether, in the absence of a confirmed Chapter 11 plan of reorganization, the Debtor Corporations (with or without insurance) would have sufficient resources to pay A-H Claims and other liabilities, whether or not currently asserted, in full when due.

In addition to A-H Claims, the Debtor Corporations are alleged to be liable, to some as yet unascertained extent, for (a) claims for damages asserted by or on behalf of owners of property in which asbestos-containing products are located, (b) claims for contribution and indemnity allegedly owing from the Debtor Corporations to other entities which have been, are being or will be sued for asbestos-related personal injury or property damage, (c) claims for personal injury or property damage arising from other products sold by the Debtor Corporations, and (d) other non-product claims (collectively the "Other Claims").

On February 5, 1983, the Debtor Corporations filed a complaint in the Bankruptcy Court petitioning the Court to estimate the number of and the value attributable to all A-H Claims against the Debtor Corporations (the "Estimation Proceeding"). Unless a consensual Chapter

11 plan is adopted, the Company believes that until the Bankruptcy Court estimates and fixes the total amount allowable for the class of contingent asbestos-health claimants, any plan of reorganization may be delayed. The Debtor Corporations have not petitioned the Bankruptcy Court for a determination of the respective rights, as among class members, to any portion of the amount so estimated or as to the merits of a particular class member's claim for relief. Determination of such rights will be made in connection with the formulation and approval process of a plan of reorganization.

In addition to the uncertainties which existed at the time the Chapter 11 proceedings were commenced, new and substantial uncertainties exist in the context of such proceedings. These uncertainties preclude any reasonable estimate at this time of the ultimate cost of the A-H Claims and Other Claims (collectively the "Claims") to the Debtor Corporations. The uncertainties include:

—the resolution of the above-referenced Estimation Proceeding;
—the method by which the A-H Claims will be satisfied;
—the effect of the Chapter 11 filing and attendant publicity on the number of Claims;
—the amount of insurance proceeds ultimately available to apply toward the disposition of the Claims once litigation pending against the Debtor Corporations' insurance carriers is resolved; and
—the method by which the Other Claims will be estimated and satisfied.

The litigation pending against the Company's insurers is discussed in this report at ITEM 3. LEGAL PROCEEDINGS.

Because of these uncertainties, the eventual disposition of the Claims cannot be predicted at this time and the ultimate loss to the Debtor Corporations, after application of estimated insurance recoveries, cannot be reasonably determined in accordance with Financial Accounting Standards Statement No. 5, "Accounting for Contingencies". Accordingly, while the ultimate liability of the Debtor Corporations could have a material adverse effect on Manville's consolidated financial position and future results of operations, no liability has been recorded in the consolidated financial statements.

Management's objectives in the Chapter 11 proceedings are to achieve the highest possible recoveries for all creditors and shareholders consistent with the Company's ability to pay and continuation of the Company's businesses. While it is possible that full recoveries will be realized, there can be no assurance at this time that the liabilities of the Debtor Corporations will not be found to exceed their assets. This could result in claims being provided for at less than 100% of their face value and the equity of the Company's common and preferred shareholders being diluted or cancelled. It is impossible at this time to predict the actual recovery which different classes of creditors and shareholders will realize.

APPENDIX E: COMPUTATION OF FINANCIAL AND INVESTMENT RATIOS

Price/Earnings Ratio (P/E)

This ratio is a number arrived at by dividing the most current twelve-months earnings per share by the final market price of the previous day.

$$\frac{\text{Most Recent Market Price}}{\substack{\text{Earnings Per Share for} \\ \text{Most Recent Twelve Months}}} = \text{Price/Earnings Ratio}$$

The following tables reflect the changes in the ratio as the factors change, assuming a starting point of $20 market price and $2 earnings per share:

Changes in Market				Changes in Earnings		
Market	Earnings	P/E		Market	Earnings	P/E
$20	$2	10		$20	$2	10
19	2	9.5		20	2.10	9.5
18	2	9		20	2.20	9.1
17	2	8.5		20	2.30	8.7
21	2	10.5		20	1.90	10.5
22	2	11		20	1.80	11.1
23	2	11.5		20	1.70	11.8
24	2	12		20	1.60	12.5

Yield

The yield of a stock as of a date is the last quarterly dividend declared—considered to be the annual rate (the quarterly rate × 4) divided by that day's market price.

$$\frac{\text{Common Stock Dividends per Year}}{\text{Most Recent Market Price}} = \text{Yield Percentage}$$

The same formula can be used for preferred stock as follows:

$$\frac{\text{Preferred Stock Dividends per Year}}{\substack{\text{Most Recent Market Price of} \\ \text{Preferred Stock}}} = \text{Preferred Stock Yield Percentage}$$

Earnings per Share

Earnings per share of the common stock must be disclosed on the face of the statement of earnings for all public companies. In its simplest form, it is computed by dividing net earnings or loss by the weighted average number of shares outstanding or considered outstanding for the period of income being reported upon, for example:

$$\frac{\substack{\text{Net Earnings for the Period (Less} \\ \text{Preferred Stock Dividends [if any])}}}{\substack{\text{Weighted Average Number of Shares} \\ \text{Outstanding}}} = \text{Earnings per Share}$$

Both the numerator of the denominator may be changed for a number of reasons, some of which are explained below. Because of the variety of matters that can alter earnings per share, comparisons between companies may be difficult.

When the statement of earnings includes extraordinary items, earnings per share must be reported before and after such extraordinary items.

Companies that have issued convertible securities, either or both bonds or preferred stock, options, warrants, or other rights that upon exercise or conversion may dilute the earnings per common share, must also compute and report primary earnings per share and fully diluted earnings per share.

Conversion might require changing the numerator by eliminating the bond interest and/or the preferred stock dividends and increasing the denominator to give effect to the contingent issuance of common stock upon the conversion, for fully diluted earnings per share.

If the company has options, warrants, or other rights that may be exercised, the denominator should be increased by the number of shares that may be issued for the diluted earnings per share.

Recognition must be given to the effect of stock dividends, splits, or reverse splits.

Return on Equity

The basic formula is to divide the net earnings by the total stockholders' equity as shown on the balance sheet.

$$\frac{\text{Net Earnings}}{\text{Stockholders' Equity}} = \text{Return on Equity Percentage}$$

There are several questions concerning the definition of net earnings for this purpose. The most common procedure is to use the bottom line of the Statement of Earnings. However, should that include extraordinary items, nonrecurring items, minority interests, discontinued operations, and preferred stock dividends? Each company decides these questions for itself, and the procedure is seldom disclosed.

There are also questions regarding stockholders' equity as used in the denominator. The amounts come directly from the balance sheet—but should you use the opening balance sheet, the ending balance sheet, the average of beginning and end, or the average for the four quarters or twelve months? It seems that the procedure used most frequently is the average of the beginning and end balance sheets.

Research and Development to Sales

This one is easy, if R & D is disclosed. Divide R & D by revenues.

$$\frac{\text{Research and Development}}{\text{Sales or Revenues}} = \text{R \& D percent of sales}$$

It should be remembered that some R & D may be performed directly on the production line and may not always be separately accounted for, since it may not always be ascertainable.

Working Capital

Working capital is the difference between Current Assets and Current Liabilities.

Depending upon the format used for the Statement of Changes in Financial Position, this amount might be shown. In some instances it is not clearly shown, but the increase or decrease during the year is shown. The amount of working capital is reported in the Financial Summary, and the important information is the trend.

Book Value per Share

Book value per share of common stock is reported by many companies in the Financial Summaries. The dollar amount of the book value per share value is the stockholders' equity as reported in the balance sheet divided by the number of shares of common stock outstanding for the end of the year.

$$\frac{\text{Stockholders' Equity}}{\text{Common Stock Share Outstanding}} = \begin{array}{c}\text{Book Value per Share of}\\ \text{Common Stock}\end{array}$$

If the company has preferred stock outstanding, the amount shown on the balance sheet is deducted from the total stockholders' equity before computing the book value per share of common stock.

Debt to Equity Ratio

This is a simple percentage resulting from dividing long-term debt (including that portion reported in current liabilities) by the sum of long-term debt and stockholders' equity, as shown in the balance sheet.

$$\frac{\text{Long-Term Debt (Including Current Portion)}}{\text{Long-Term Debt Plus Stockholders' Equity}} = \text{Debt to Equity Ratio}$$

There could be a number of variations of this computation if the amounts are significant. The following items could be added to both the numerator and denominator:

    Short-term debt other than current portion of long-term debt
    Capital lease obligations
    Deferred taxes
    Deferred pension costs.

Depreciation to Fixed Assets Ratio

This ratio percentage is computed by dividing the accumulated depreciation, depletion, and amortization of property by the property, plant, and equipment (other than land) as reported on the balance sheet. The details are frequently reported in the Notes to Financial Statements.

$$\frac{\text{Accumulated Depreciation, etc.}}{\text{Property, Plant, and Equipment}} = \begin{array}{c}\text{Depreciation to Fixed Assets}\\ \text{Percentage}\end{array}$$

Profit Margin

Dividing net income by sales and operating revenues results in the profit margin often used by management.

$$\frac{\text{Net Income}}{\text{Sales and Operating Revenues}} = \text{Profit Margin Percentage}$$

Net income is from continuing operations and before extraordinary items and minority interest.

APPENDIX F: FMC ANNUAL REPORT, 1981

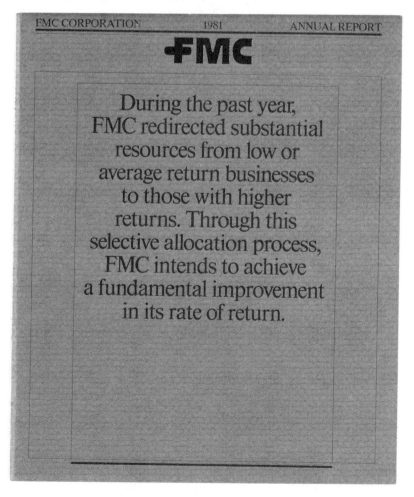

FMC CORPORATION 1981 ANNUAL REPORT

FMC

During the past year, FMC redirected substantial resources from low or average return businesses to those with higher returns. Through this selective allocation process, FMC intends to achieve a fundamental improvement in its rate of return.

Stockholder data

Annual meeting of stockholders
FMC's annual meeting of stockholders will be held at 3:00 p.m. on Friday, April 23, 1982 at 200 East Randolph Drive, Chicago, Illinois.

Notice of the meeting, together with proxy material, will be mailed to stockholders of record approximately 40 days prior to the meeting.

Stockholder services
Stockholders' questions about their FMC common or preferred stock should be addressed to:

FMC Corporation
Stockholder Services Department
200 East Randolph Drive
Chicago, Illinois 60601

Dividend reinvestment
FMC offers its stockholders an Automatic Dividend Reinvestment Service. Dividends on both common and preferred stock may be reinvested. For more information, contact FMC's Stockholder Services Department.

Transfer agents
FMC Corporation
Stockholder Services Department
200 East Randolph Drive
Chicago, Illinois 60601

Citibank, N.A.
111 Wall Street
New York, New York 10043

Registrars of stock
Continental Illinois National Bank and Trust Company of Chicago
Chicago, Illinois

Citibank, N.A.
New York, New York

Principal market of common stock and $3.25 preferred stock
New York Stock Exchange
New York, New York

Form 10-K
A copy of the company's Annual Report to the Securities and Exchange Commission on Form 10-K for 1981 is available upon written request to:

FMC Corporation
Public Relations Department
200 East Randolph Drive
Chicago, Illinois 60601

FMC Corporation 53rd Annual Report

As one of the world's leading producers of machinery and chemicals for industry, agriculture and government, FMC participates on a worldwide basis in selected segments of five broad markets: Industrial Chemicals, Petroleum Equipment and Services, Defense Equipment and Systems, Performance Chemicals and Specialized Machinery. FMC operates 129 manufacturing facilities and mines in 29 states and 14 foreign countries.

Contents

To our Stockholders and Employees:
In last year's annual report, I discussed our plan to increase FMC's return on equity to 18 percent during the decade of the 1980's.

Setting a corporation of the size and complexity of FMC on a new course is neither an easy task, nor one that can be accomplished quickly, but our objectives are not short-term. We intend to establish a new, higher level of profitability for FMC, which will allow the company to be more responsive to the challenges of the future. We expect that the future will be characterized by more volatile business cycles, high inflation rates and growing competition for increasingly scarce human and financial resources.

The two primary strategies we are following are 1) concentrating our capital and nonfinancial resources in the businesses we believe will produce consistent high returns over the long term, and 2) withdrawing from businesses that clearly cannot make an acceptable contribution to reaching our ambitious objectives. The most important actions taken during 1981 are highlighted on pages 8-19 of this annual report. The financial payoff from many of these actions will not be apparent until 1982, or even later in some cases, but we believe substantial progress was made in 1981 toward implementing the strategies we established several years ago.

One strategic move during 1981 that had a measurable and very noticeable impact was the sale of FMC's Power Transmission Group. The power transmission business was basically sound and well-managed, but it operated in a mature, slow-growth industry and did not have a strong technological orientation. This sale is a major step in concentrating our capital

Financial Summary

(Dollars in millions, except per share data)	1981	1980*	Change
Sales of continuing operations:			
In the United States	$ 2,192.4	$ 2,179.2	+1%
Outside the United States	1,174.3	1,428.0	+14%
Total	$ 3,366.7	$ 3,307.2	+5%
Income from continuing operations:			
Before income taxes	$ 256.7	$ 170.5	+51%
After income taxes	$ 176.5	$ 140.7	+25%
Percent of sales	5.2%	4.4%	
Income (loss) from discontinued operations (after tax)	$ (37.0)	$ 2.0	
Net income	$ 139.5	$ 142.7	–2%
Earnings per common share—primary:			
Continuing operations	$ 5.28	$ 4.20	+26%
Discontinued operations	$ (1.13)	.06	
Net Income	$ 4.15	$ 4.26	–3%
Earnings per common share—fully diluted:			
Continuing operations	$ 4.88	$ 3.88	+26%
Discontinued operations	$ (1.01)	.05	
Net Income	$ 3.87	$ 3.93	–2%
Dividends per share:			
Common	$ 1.60	$ 1.45	+10%
Stock price range:			
Common	$ 35¾–24⅞	$ 31½–21½	

*Restated for discontinued operations.

1

and nonfinancial resources in businesses that will improve FMC's future profitability.

Financial results

Sales from continuing operations of $3.4 billion grew 5 percent in 1981, and net income of $139.5 million decreased 2 percent. Net income includes the negative effect of the Power Transmission Group divestiture.

The results of FMC's continuing operations, the basis of our future performance, showed satisfactory progress by any measure. Earnings from continuing operations increased 25 percent to $5.28 per share, and represented a record level of earnings for FMC. The after-tax margin on sales for continuing operations increased to 5.2 percent, from 4.4 percent the prior year, despite an increase in the tax rate to 31.2 percent from 17.5 percent.

Return on equity for our continuing operations improved from 11.7 percent in 1980 to 13.9 percent in 1981. While return on equity is conventionally calculated on the basis of net income, we believe a better measure of FMC's progress is the return on equity of continuing operations.

The sale of the Power Transmission Group for $125 million, combined with provision for the expected divestiture of the Outdoor Power Equipment Division in 1982, resulted in a write-off of $36.8 million, or $1.13 per share, including approximately $21 million of goodwill written-off without tax benefit. This loss is reflected in FMC's net income.

Partially offsetting the negative impact of discontinued operations was an earnings increase resulting from the adoption of Statement of Financial Accounting Standards No. 52—Foreign Currency Translation (SFAS 52). The effect of SFAS 52 was to increase 1981 net income by $17.5 million, or $.54 per share. This accounting change removes the obscuring effect of changing currency translation rates from the financial results of most foreign operations, and it more accurately reflects their operating performance in FMC's consolidated financial statements. A more complete description of SFAS 52 and its effect on FMC's earnings is contained in Note 2 of the financial statements.

Financial position

FMC's financial position remained sound in 1981. Long-term debt accounted for 23 percent of total capital at year-end compared to 25 percent a year ago. The percentage of long-term debt in the capital structure has now declined for six consecutive years. Utilization of working capital by FMC's operations improved substantially in 1981. Operating working capital, consisting of inventories and trade receivables, less trade payables and accrued liabilities, decreased $61 million, or 20 percent, from year-end 1980. Operating working capital as a percent of sales decreased to 7.2 cents at year-end 1980. Cash and marketable securities increased to $219.3 million, from $126.8 million at the end of 1980. This increase resulted from receipt of the proceeds from the Power Transmission Group divestiture in October, 1981. Divestiture proceeds aside, the corporation was self-financing in 1981 and reduced total debt by $13.4 million.

Financial reporting

To communicate our objectives and allow you to better measure our progress toward them, we have changed the presentation of our industry segment data, which is the format we use in discussing FMC's operating results. Effective with this year's annual report, we will report our results in five industry segments: industrial chemicals, petroleum equipment and services, defense equipment and systems, performance chemicals, and specialized machinery.

Each of our businesses has a unique and essential role to play in helping us reach our objectives, and this revised segmentation groups together businesses with similar strategic roles. Some of our businesses are in a high-growth stage, and they will receive the necessary capital and non-financial resources to ensure their continued growth. Other of our businesses are self-financing, high-return businesses which we manage with the objective of providing the resources required by the higher-growth segments. This ongoing process of selectively channeling our resources is the key to achieving the higher-return objectives we have set for FMC.

Safety

In 1977, we established a companywide program to reemphasize our commitment to employee safety. Since then, we have cut the rate of serious accidents at our plants by more than half. As a result of companywide efforts, we have earned the National Safety Council's Award of Honor, the highest award given by the Council. Of more than 6,000 manufacturing companies and plants that report to the National Safety Council, only 5 percent have received the Award of Honor. We take a great deal of pride in this accomplishment.

Management changes

Several important changes in FMC's top management occurred in 1981. Charles H. Johnson, General Manager of the Defense Equipment Group, and W. Glenn Bush, General Manager of the Material Handling Group, were elected Vice Presidents of the corporation. Both were appointed to their present positions in 1980.

James A. McClung was appointed Director of International Business, and was also elected a Vice President during 1981. He is responsible for overall corporate policy relating to FMC's international business. Prior to assuming his present duties, Mr. McClung was General Manager of the Alkali Chemicals Division. Robert McLellan, who was responsible for both international business and government affairs, is now devoting full time to the increasingly important area of government affairs and has relocated to Washington, D.C.

Daniel C. Smith, Vice President and General Counsel, retired during 1981, and his duties have been assumed by Patrick J. Head, also elected a Vice President, who joined FMC in 1981.

Donald C. Oskin, Executive Vice President, will retire on March 1, 1982, after 36 years of service. He has been an officer of FMC for 20 years and became Executive Vice President, responsible for marketing, in 1967. His personal attention to assuring good relations with our major customers has contributed greatly to establishing FMC's strong position in many of our most important markets. We will miss having the benefit of Mr. Oskin's knowledge and long experience.

Outlook

For the third consecutive year, it is necessary to express concern about the course of the worldwide economy and its impact on our markets. The current U.S. recession is expected by many to be as severe as the 1974-75 downturn, and we are planning accordingly.

In spite of the dim economic outlook, several of our major businesses are unlikely to be significantly affected by the recession. Our defense equipment business is assured of growth in sales and earnings in 1982 as production of Bradley Fighting Vehicles accelerates. With full-scale production of fighting vehicles, defense equipment sales should exceed $1 billion in 1982.

Our petroleum equipment business is expected to continue to grow rapidly, and new manufacturing capacity for that business is either in place or coming on-line. While growth in drilling activity will probably slow in 1982, we expect that there will be more deep, high-pressure wells completed, which will directly benefit our wellhead equipment operations.

For performance chemicals, results normally depend on noneconomic factors. Pest pressures and weather conditions are key variables, since the majority of this FMC business area is related to agriculture. In 1982, however, continued high interest rates, declining farm income and depressed commodity prices cause us to take a cautious view of farmers' willingness and ability to plant aggressively and buy products, such as ours, that increase the productivity of farmland. Our domestic performance chemicals business may decline in 1982, but we have substantial market penetration opportunities outside the United States that should offset a decline in our domestic business.

Both the industrial chemical and specialized machinery markets will be affected by general economic conditions. These FMC businesses have been operating in an uncertain and recessionary environment for almost two years. Given the economic environment, the industrial chemicals business has been extraordinarily successful. However, we do not believe it can continue to generate earnings gains in 1982.

The specialized machinery business should continue to perform in line with the capital goods sector of the economy, which implies a late 1982 recovery and a likely decline in earnings for the year.

Our current consolidated forecast projects growth in both sales and earnings in 1982, but the severity of the recession and continuation of high interest rates make our performance for the year difficult to project with accuracy. We are dedicated to a program of tight cost controls and improved manufacturing capabilities. We will continue our commitments to increasing research and development expenditures, and we anticipate increased capital investment in 1982 to prepare for the future opportunities that we believe exist for FMC.

[signature]

Robert H. Malott
Chairman of the Board
and Chief Executive Officer

February 24, 1982

Sales from continuing operations (Dollars in millions)

Income from continuing operations (Dollars in millions)

Return on equity from continuing operations (Percent)

Review of Operations

Sales of FMC's continuing operations increased $160 million, or 5 percent, to $3.4 billion. Operating profit before tax of $311 million, on the same basis, increased $64 million, or 26 percent, from the prior year with three of FMC's five industry segments reporting gains.

Effective with this year's annual report, FMC's industry segments have been restructured to more accurately reflect our management emphasis. Prior years' data have been restated accordingly. At the end of the third quarter, FMC's former Power Transmission Group was sold, and provision was made for the eventual disposition of the

Outdoor Power Equipment Division. These businesses are classified as discontinued operations, and their sales and earnings are not included in the industry segment data for 1981 or prior years.

Industrial Chemicals

Sales increased 11 percent, and earnings improved 22 percent,

reflecting profit margin gains in most major operations.

Sales and earnings of alkali chemicals increased with gains in natural soda ash and caustic soda. Sales of caustic soda increased sharply as a result of continued strong demand and higher selling prices. Manufacturing process improvements and cost reduction efforts contributed to higher margins.

Soda ash shipments were about the same as in 1980, although demand from the glass market, the biggest single user of soda ash, was weak. Despite lower demand and higher industry capacity, FMC improved its domestic market position, accounting for more than 30

percent of total U.S. sales. Earnings volume declined, reflecting recessionary conditions in many foreign countries, but FMC export shipments continued to represent more than one-third of total U.S. soda ash exports.

Installation of the first long-wall mining machine at the Green River, Wyoming soda ash facility was accomplished during 1981, and initial production results are encouraging. Startup of the Lawrence, Kansas test facility at Green River also began during the year.

Sales of phosphorus chemicals increased strongly, and profit margins improved. The primary source of growth in both sales and earnings was a higher operating rate resulting from improved electric power availability at the Pocatello, Idaho elemental phosphorus plant, which provides the raw material for the entire phosphorus product line. Power availability from local sources was better than in 1980, and supplemental power was purchased from other sources during the normal summer curtailment period. The higher cost of supplemental power was more than offset by the manufacturing efficiencies arising from a higher level of capacity utilization.

Sales of sodium tripolyphosphate, FMC's most important

phosphorus product, increased, although some softness in demand was evident during the latter part of the year. Good increases were also recorded in sales of phosphoric acid, food grade phosphates, and phosphorus pentasulfide. Phosphorus pentasulfide, introduced last year, is the most recent addition to FMC's phosphorus line.

Operations at the new phosphorus pentasulfide plant at Lawrence, Kansas are going smoothly, but weak market conditions kept the plant from reaching its targeted output.

Specialty chemical sales increased moderately, but earnings were substantially above the 1980 level. Above average growth continued in hydrogen peroxide, and higher levels of capacity utilization at the South Charleston, West Virginia and Bayport, Texas plants allowed profit margins to expand. Late in 1981, a 33 percent expansion of the Bayport plant was announced. The expansion will bring the plant's capacity to 80 million pounds per year, and FMC's total hydrogen peroxide capacity will rise to 183 million pounds per year. In addition, the expansion project includes process improvements that will result in substantial manufacturing cost reduction.

Sales of chlorinated dry bleaches increased substantially, and excellent manufacturing cost performance and

tight control of overhead expenses led to a sharp increase in margins. Sales and earnings of plasticizers and fluid additive products also increased, recovering from weak market conditions in 1980.

Foret S.A., FMC's Spanish subsidiary, reported strong sales growth as the volume of most products increased and selling prices were higher. Earnings also improved, but profit margins declined due to higher costs for energy and raw materials that were not fully offset by selling price increases. Raw material costs will improve in 1982, when Foret completes construction of its own sulfuric acid plant, which will provide a stable, low-cost source of this key raw material.

Petroleum Equipment and Services

Sales increased 44 percent, and earnings rose 69 percent. Sales growth paralleled the 1981 increase in worldwide petroleum industry exploration and production spending. Margins expanded in response to a high level of capacity utilization and more efficient manufacturing operations resulting from the addition of a new plant and equipment. Despite increased capacity, backlog grew 25 percent, to $210 million at year-end.

Wellhead equipment sales increased more than 50 percent in 1981, as drilling activity

continued the strong upward trend of recent years. The average number of drilling rigs in operation in the United States increased 21 percent to 3,969 rigs, and U.S. well completions increased 21 percent. Foreign drilling activity also increased again, although Canadian activity declined, and the world fleet of offshore drilling rigs was fully utilized during the year.

Sales of fluid control products also grew significantly as a result of the higher level of drilling activity and a significant increase in stimulation of both new and existing wells. Higher market prices for U.S. oil led to dramatic growth in the work over and servicing of existing wells, and this market is a heavy user of fluid control products.

Capital expenditures for petroleum equipment and services totaled $46.3 million in 1981, an increase of 45 percent. A new plant for fluid control products was opened at Stephenville, Texas during the first half of 1981 and an existing fluid control plant at Brea, California was expanded. A doubling of FMC's wellhead equipment plant in Singapore was begun late in 1981 and is now approaching completion. More information on these projects is contained on pages 12 and 13.

Operations by Industry Segments

(Dollars in millions)	1981	1980*	1979*	1978*	1977*
Sales					
Industrial Chemicals	$ 948.3	$ 856.8	$ 762.3	$ 680.2	$ 582.4
Petroleum Equipment and Services	340.0	236.4	172.7	148.5	121.0
Defense Equipment and Systems	582.0	570.4	462.9	447.9	299.6
Performance Chemicals	434.4	362.1	366.1	312.6	213.2
Specialized Machinery	1,086.5	1,199.2	1,267.0	1,100.7	894.9
Eliminations	(24.5)	(17.7)	(12.6)	(16.7)	(14.5)
Total	$3,366.7	$3,207.2	$3,018.4	$2,673.2	$2,096.6
Operating results					
Industrial Chemicals	$ 140.7	$ 115.6	$ 86.6	$ 84.3	$ 113.2
Petroleum Equipment and Services	69.0	41.0	26.9	24.4	21.2
Defense Equipment and Systems	53.4	71.7	61.1	51.0	40.0
Performance Chemicals	54.3	(2.4)	32.3	32.5	15.3
Specialized Machinery	(5.5)	20.6	38.2	69.0	49.1
Eliminations	(1.1)	0.2	0.4	(0.6)	—
Total	$ 310.8	$ 246.7	$ 245.5	$ 260.6	$ 238.8

*Restated for discontinued operations and realignment of industry segments.

Industrial Chemicals sales
(Dollars in millions)

operating profits
(Dollars in millions)

Petroleum Equipment and Services sales
(Dollars in millions)

operating profits
(Dollars in millions)

Defense Equipment and Systems

Sales rose 2 percent from the 1980 level as a moderate increase from tracked vehicle operations was partly offset by lower sales of naval ordnance equipment. Earnings declined 26 percent, primarily due to an 11-week strike at the San Jose, California vehicle production facility.

Sales from military tracked vehicle operations increased despite the San Jose strike. Strong pre-strike production of M113 family vehicles and initial deliveries of the first production units of M2 and M3 Bradley Fighting Vehicles (BFV) contributed to sales growth. Strike costs and start-up expenses associated with the production of fighting vehicles lowered earnings for the year.

Congress has approved the Army's fiscal year 1982 budget request for 600 fighting vehicles, and material procurement for the vehicles is now under contract. In addition, a supplemental appropriation for an additional 100 vehicles was approved for fiscal year 1981 procurement. In addition to the material procurement contract for fiscal year 1982, FMC currently has contracts to manufacture 500 fighting vehicles and 48 units of the first BFV derivative, a carrier for the Army's new Multiple Launch Rocket System. These contracts total approximately $1 billion.

Sales of naval ordnance equipment declined moderately from the record level of 1980, due to year-to-year timing differences in the delivery of major ordnance systems. Deliveries of Mark 13 guided missile launching systems and Mark 75 gun mounts declined from 1980, when several large contracts were completed. Due to the long manufacturing cycle for these types of products, shipment of completed units tends to cluster toward the end of each contract. Sales should increase substantially in 1982, when systems now in production are completed and shipped.

Production of a new naval ordnance product was begun in 1981 with the receipt of a $20 million contract for Armored Box Launching Systems capable of launching Tomahawk and Harpoon cruise missiles. These systems will be included in the retrofitting of the U.S. Navy's battleship New Jersey.

Defense equipment and systems operations ended the year with a backlog of $2.0 billion, an increase of 64 percent from year-end 1980.

Performance Chemicals

Sales increased 20 percent and earnings rebounded sharply from the loss reported in 1980. Agricultural chemical sales grew 22 percent, compared to 1980, and exceeded the record 1979 level by 14 percent. Higher volume and better manufacturing efficiency led to a substantial earnings recovery from the depressed results of the prior year. Sales of Furadan® insecticide-nematicide, FMC's largest selling proprietary agricultural chemical product, improved substantially, with especially strong international performance. Investments in international marketing and distribution made in prior years are now paying off as international sales of Furadan increased more than 65 percent. During 1981, new U.S. Furadan registrations were received for soybeans, sorghum, grapes, wheat, cotton, barley and oats. In addition, international marketing of Marshall® insecticide, a Furadan derivative, was begun. A U.S. registration for Marshall is expected in 1984.

Sales of synthetic pyrethroid products increased approximately 50 percent, recovering from extremely weak market conditions in 1980, when widespread drought damaged cotton crops throughout the western hemisphere. More normal weather conditions in 1981 led to a strong increase in U.S. sales of Pounce® insecticide, and international sales were aided by the introduction of Arrivo® pyrethroid insecticide, a second-generation synthetic pyrethroid. Sales of DV ester, a key raw material used in the production of synthetic pyrethroids, were up over 50 percent. Proprietary process technology for the manufacture of DV ester has allowed FMC to establish a leading position in this market.

Emphasis on research and development programs for proprietary agricultural chemical products continued at a high level in 1981. Research and development expenditures increased nearly 25 percent, and a major new research facility in Princeton, New Jersey is now nearing completion.

Sales of food and pharmaceutical additives grew 28 percent in 1981, and profit margins improved again. Sales of FMC's proprietary Avicel® microcrystalline cellulose increased strongly, led by rapid penetration of the European market for pharmaceutical additives. Strong growth of European sales allowed the two-year-old Avicel plant in Ireland to achieve a high level of capacity utilization which contributed significantly to profit margin improvement. Substantial growth was also reported in hydrocolloid products, and sales and earnings reached record levels.

Specialized Machinery

Sales declined 9 percent from 1980, due almost entirely to lower railcar shipments, and a loss was reported for the year. Improved food machinery operations and construction equipment operations were offset by lower earnings from material handling and special products operations.

Food machinery sales grew 8 percent, and earnings increased more rapidly. A realignment of manufacturing facilities, which hurt earnings in 1980, is now beginning to pay off in higher profit margins, particularly in food processing and agricultural machinery operations. Higher sales and earnings in citrus machinery operations, and inclusion of a full year's operating results for the Beverage Equipment Division, which was acquired in May, 1980, also contributed to the strong food machinery performance.

Sales of construction equipment increased 5 percent, but a loss was reported for the year. Through tighter control of manufacturing and overhead costs, the 1981 loss was cut from the prior year. The construction equipment market remained depressed for the second consecutive year, and North American retail unit volume of cranes and excavators declined nearly 15 percent. A virtual depression in the construction industry has been caused by high interest rates and a stagnant U.S. economy. In a cyclically declining market, FMC held or improved its market share in eight of its ten construction equipment product lines.

Sales and earnings from material handling operations declined in 1981, primarily due to a substantial decline in railcar production. The railcar market is undergoing its worst cyclical decline since the late 1940's. FMC halted railcar manufacture in October, when the backlog was exhausted, and production is not expected to resume before the second half of 1982. Airline equipment sales and earnings also declined, since this operation, located in San Jose, was also involved in the previously mentioned 11-week strike which disrupted military equipment production. All other material handling operations reported higher earnings, with especially strong results in the material handling equipment and systems businesses.

Special products sales were about the same as in 1980, but earnings declined. Lower earnings were recorded by sweeper and automotive service equipment operations, partly offset by gains in turbo pump operations.

During 1981, the Engineered Systems Division and several smaller material handling businesses were sold, but these divestitures did not have a material impact on the segment's results.

Raymond C. Tower
President and Chief
Operating Officer

Defense Equipment and Systems

sales
(Dollars in millions)

operating profits
(Dollars in millions)

Performance Chemicals

sales
(Dollars in millions)

operating profits
(Dollars in millions)

Specialized Machinery

sales
(Dollars in millions)

operating profits
(Dollars in millions)

149

SELECTIVE ALLOCATION OF RESOURCES

Strategy

At FMC's 1980 annual meeting, a goal of 18 percent return on equity for the corporation was announced. Through a multi-year shifting of assets from low- or average-return businesses to high-return businesses, the company will achieve a fundamental improvement in its rate of return.

We will support high-return businesses while maintaining strong positions in other, lower-return businesses that provide immediate cash flow to support growth. Each FMC business will receive the resources required to play its role in helping the corporation reach its objectives. Those business units that clearly cannot make a satisfactory contribution to helping the corporation achieve its long-term goals will be candidates for divestiture.

A major strategic element of our plan is the allocation of research and development funds and capital expenditures. FMC's goal is to allocate more than 75 percent annually of our research and development and capital spending to high-return businesses for capacity expansion, cost reduction and product development. We believe 1981 was a vintage year for high-return projects—projects that will help carry FMC toward its goal

of 18 percent return on equity. The projects and programs depicted below, and discussed in the pages that follow, represent the most important actions taken in 1981 to raise FMC's return on equity.

There were, of course, many other capital investment projects either begun or completed; other new products brought to market; and other less visible but equally important changes in manufacturing methods and technologies, management systems, and the managerial approach to certain businesses and markets which are not shown. ∎∎∎

(Dollars in millions)	Capital expenditures 1981		Research and development expenditures 1981	
Industrial Chemicals	42.6%	$115.6	25.4%	$26.9
Petroleum Equipment and Services	17.0%	46.3	5.1%	5.4
Defense Equipment and Systems	13.5%	38.1	6.0%	6.4
Performance Chemicals	7.9%	21.4	31.3%	33.1
Specialized Machinery	13.1%	35.7	28.0%	29.6
Corporate	6.3%	17.1	4.2%	4.4
Total	100.0%	$272.2	100.0%	$105.8

Implementation

The elements in determining return on equity are net margin, asset turnover and financial leverage. The projects and programs highlighted in this annual report are intended to raise FMC's return on equity through either increased net margin or faster asset turnover for the corporation. These projects have no effect on financial leverage, since they have been financed with internally generated cash flows. In fact, FMC's return on equity for continuing operations increased in 1981, despite a decline in financial leverage.

The accompanying table shows how each project is expected to contribute to a higher return on equity for FMC. Initially, these investments may actually reduce net margins or asset turnover for the business units responsible for them, either because of start-up expenses or a low initial rate of capacity utilization. Off-setting whatever negative effect may be associated with these investment, or individual businesses, however, is the beneficial effect of concentrating FMC's operating assets in those businesses with the highest net margin and/or fastest asset turnover. Even though the financial performance of some individual businesses may suffer temporarily, FMC's return on equity will benefit.

Also shown in the table is the intended effect of each investment on the marketplace. There is an appropriate balance between new product investments to ensure future high returns and investments that build on existing positions in high-return businesses. ∎∎∎

	Expected financial results		Market share	
	Increase net margin	Increase asset turnover	New product or market	Increase or maintain market share
Bradley Fighting Vehicles				
New defense equipment plant				
New petroleum equipment capacity				
New agricultural chemical products				
New research facility				
New sulfuric acid plant				
Longwall and solution mining				
Gold mining venture				
New airline equipment plant				
Divestitures				

Longwall mining system installed

First Bradley Fighting Vehicles delivered

Construction of new defense equipment plant begun

Solution mining test continues

New fluid control equipment plant opened

Construction of sulfuric acid plant begun

Wellhead equipment plant expanded

New proprietary agricultural chemicals introduced

First gold at Jerritt Canyon produced

New research facility nears completion

Construction of new airline equipment plant started

Divestitures

The Bradley Fighting Vehicle (BFV) System is FMC's newest defense equipment product line, and it will soon become the largest as well.

The system consists of the M2 Infantry Fighting Vehicle, M3 Cavalry Fighting Vehicle and a universal carrier which can be adapted to multiple uses. After more than four years of development and testing, initial vehicle deliveries began in 1981, and they will accelerate to a rate of 50 vehicles per month by early 1983. Rapid increases in BFV deliveries will help push FMC's defense equipment sales to more than $1 billion in 1982.

Highly mobile and sophisti-cated, the M2 and M3 can travel at speeds up to 42 miles per hour, deliver unprecedented fire power and swim rivers. FMC fighting vehicles have proven themselves in over 18 months of tests to be the most formidable infantry and cavalry fighting machines ever built.

Protected by FMC's proprietary spaced laminate armor, the vehicles are armed with a 25 mm automatic cannon, TOW missile launcher system, and a 7.62 mm machine gun. In addition to a commander, driver, and gunner, the M2 carries six infantrymen, while the M3 carries two cavalrymen. Both are designed to provide maximum support for the M1 main battle tank.

Current Army plans anticipate procurement of 6,882 M2 and M3 fighting vehicles by fiscal 1989, with an estimated sales value to FMC of nearly $5 billion. Contracts received to date total approximately $1 billion for the production of 500 M2 and M3 vehicles, 48 units of the universal carrier adapted to transport the Army's Multiple Launch Rocket System, and procurement of materials for an additional 600 M2's and M3's. The vehicles currently under contract are scheduled to be delivered by May, 1984.

New production capacity

FMC has invested more than $50 million in plant and equipment to produce fighting vehicles at San Jose, California. An FMC plant at Aiken, South Carolina is now being converted and enlarged at a cost of approximately $25 million to support production of tracked vehicles. The facility will manufacture parts for assembly in San Jose. Completion of the 190,000-square-foot plant is expected by late 1982.

Based on FMC's 20 years of experience with the M113 family of tracked vehicles, there is good reason to expect that the BFV will become a family of related vehicles derived from the basic M2 chassis. The M113 family, for example, includes 18 models, and total production now exceeds 65,000 units, compared to an originally projected requirement of only 4,000 units.

The first derivative vehicle in the BFV family, a carrier for the Multiple Launch Rocket System, is already in production. With the development of additional derivatives, several of which are already in the planning stage, total production of Bradley Fighting Vehicles could exceed 12,000 units.

At Aiken, South Carolina, FMC is converting and enlarging an existing related facility to support production of military tracked vehicles. (left)

The U. S. Army plans to buy 6,882 Bradley Fighting Vehicles during the 1980's. Their unprecedented mobility and firepower will enable infantrymen to either launch a mounted attack under armor protection or to dismount from the vehicle and fight on foot. (below right)

FMC's newest defense equipment product—the Bradley Fighting Vehicle—has demonstrated outstanding performance and reliability during testing at Camp Roberts, California. (below left)

FMC's petroleum equipment sales have nearly doubled in the past two years, and continuing growth at above average rates is expected.

To accommodate this rapid growth, FMC is engaged in a multiyear capacity expansion program. During the past three years, capital expenditures in petroleum equipment operations totaled $93 million, and expenditures in the 1982-83 period will be even greater.

During 1981, a new fluid control plant was opened at Stephenville, Texas, and major expansions of fluid control and wellhead equipment plants in Brea, California and Singapore were begun.

Stephenville, Texas In March, FMC opened a new fluid control equipment manufacturing facility in Stephenville, Texas. The 120,000-square-foot plant produces flow control products for oil and gas drilling and well servicing applications. The plant's principal product line is unions which are used to connect high pressure piping. FMC holds the dominant market position in these products. The highly automated plant will become one of only a few "Class A" manufacturing

Expansion of FMC's wellhead equipment plant in Singapore will double its manufacturing capacity to support increased drilling activity in Southeast Asia. (right)

To increase manufacturing capacity for Longsweep® swivel joints, FMC installed new machine tools and material handling equipment, including robotics, shown here, at its Brea, California plant. (left)

FMC's second new petroleum equipment plant in two years was opened in Stephenville, Texas, to produce fluid control products. Highly automated, the plant will become one of only a few "Class A" manufacturing plants in the United States during 1982. (below)

plants in the United States during 1982. "Class A" status requires that the plant conform to 20 demanding performance standards including meeting its delivery schedules at least 95 percent of the time.

By relocating the union product line from FMC's Houston plant to Stephenville, additional manufacturing capacity for further expansion of oilfield products is now available in Houston.

Brea, California New machine tools and material handling equipment, including robotics, were installed at FMC's Brea plant to meet manufacturing capacity for another fluid control product, Longsweep® swivel joints. FMC holds the leading market position in swivel joints, which are essential components in flexible metal piping used by oilfield service companies and drilling contractors. The new equipment at Brea is being used in a 35,000-square-foot addition which was completed in 1980.

Singapore As a result of the worldwide increase in drilling activity, FMC's wellhead equipment plant in Singapore underwent a major expansion in 1981 that will approximately double its manufacturing capacity. Wellhead equipment provides the means for supporting and sealing casing and tubing, and for controlling the flow of oil or gas from a producing well. FMC is one of the largest suppliers of wellhead equipment in the world.

The 32,500-square-foot plant expansion will nearly double the Singapore facility's plant and office space needed to support strong growth in the Southeast Asian market. The expansion was completed during the first quarter of 1982.

13

12

FMC began international marketing of two new products — Arrivo® pyrethroid insecticide and Marshall® insecticide — in 1981.

New proprietary products are essential to the future of the agricultural chemical business. A continuing flow of new products is needed to replace existing products as they mature and to build on the distribution channels in which FMC has made a significant investment.

Arrivo is a new, second-generation synthetic pyrethroid product that is being marketed in Latin America and Africa. FMC is among the leaders in the development and marketing of synthetic pyrethroids, a new

class of pesticides that are more efficacious and environmentally more desirable than the older products that they are replacing. Arrivo is similar to FMC's Pounce® insecticide, also a synthetic pyrethroid, but Arrivo provides greater efficacy. It is primarily used to combat pests that attack cotton, but it is also effective on coffee, soybeans, and a wide variety of vegetables.

Marshall is an analog of Furadan® insecticide-nematicide, FMC's largest selling agricultural chemical product.

It is opening new markets where FMC does not hold the patent rights to Furadan and on crops where low-toxicity spray application is required, such as apples and citrus.

The spectrum of activity, improved cost-effectiveness and lower toxicity of Arrivo and Marshall will give them a broad range of applicability. Both products are expected to be registered in the United States in 1984.

Agricultural chemical research

Construction was essentially completed during 1981 on a new agricultural chemical research facility in Princeton, New Jersey. The $30-million

project consolidates existing research facilities in Princeton and Middleport, New York, and it will double FMC's basic discovery effort to increase the flow of new proprietary pesticides beyond the mid-1980's. The continuing development of new proprietary products through research is a critical success factor in the agricultural chemical business.

Discovery of new compounds which are both effective pest control agents and economic to produce is a difficult, highly technical process. Based on average industry experience, screening 15,000 compounds yields only one success. By doubling the number of com-

pounds screened, a commensurate increase in the number of successful new products is expected. Furthermore, new products should have a higher level of profitability, since the necessary investment in marketing and distribution systems has already been made.

As the largest single capital investment FMC has ever made in a research facility, the Princeton expansion will add 227,000 square feet to an existing 300,000 square feet of research facilities on a 163-acre site. Along with the latest in laboratory facilities, the expansion includes 31,000 square feet of greenhouses.

153

To further strengthen FMC's leadership position in the natural soda ash industry, two new cost reduction technologies are being tested and developed for mining trona ore—the raw material for natural soda ash.

FMC is the largest and lowest-cost producer of natural soda ash in the world with 2.8 million tons of annual capacity.

Longwall mining In March, FMC installed its first longwall mining system. Longwall mining is used extensively in coal mines, but coal mining equipment is not suitable for use in the harder shale found in trona deposits. FMC sponsored

the development of more costly, higher-quality equipment. The longwall method of mining will increase by 50 percent the amount of trona recovered compared to conventional mining techniques and substantially reduce underground mining costs.

By conventional mining, only about 45 percent of the ore is removed, and the remainder is left in the form of pillars to sup-

port the roof. The longwall unit has a hydraulic roof support system that advances with the unit. After the ore is removed, the roof support system moves forward, and the roof is allowed to collapse. The longwall unit is expected to have an ore recovery rate of almost 70 percent.

By the mid-1980's, FMC will have two longwall units operating at full capacity, and they should be able to produce 40 percent of the Green River plant's annual trona ore requirement of more than five million tons. The longwall units will replace many of the more costly conventional mining operations.

Solution mining During 1981, FMC began testing new technology for the solution mining of trona. While solution mining is widely used to extract other minerals, it has never before been attempted in trona. FMC will spend more than $30 million to test this technology over the next several years.

Potentially a major technological breakthrough, the process involves injecting a solution into the trona bed by means of a well to dissolve the ore underground. The trona-bearing solution is then pumped to the surface through a second well for processing. If successful, this process could dramatically reduce costs by eliminating men

and machines underground, and by simplifying the refining process. It would also make possible the recovery of trona reserves at depths that are uneconomical to mine by conventional means.

A major backward-integration project to produce sulfuric acid at Foret, FMC's large Spanish subsidiary, was begun during 1981.

The new 300,000-metric-ton-per-year plant is scheduled for start-up by fall of 1982. The plant will utilize locally available pyrites as the source of

Construction of a 393,000-metric-ton-per-year sulfuric-acid plant in Spain will ensure a steady, low-cost supply of this essential raw material which is used to produce phosphates. (left)

At FMC's trona mine in Green River, Wyoming, installation of a longwall mining machine will increase the recovery of trona by 50 percent compared to conventional mining techniques. (below left)

Solution mining of trona ore is being tested at a pilot plant in Wyoming. Successful development of the new mining process could greatly reduce the cost of producing soda ash. (below right)

sulfur, significantly reducing manufacturing costs and eliminating the wide fluctuations in the cost of sulfur.

Sulfuric acid is a key raw material used by Foret to produce phosphates, which comprise approximately half of its sales. The new plant will ensure a continuing, stable supply of low-cost sulfuric acid, and it will make Foret the low-cost producer of phosphates compared to other European producers. This low-cost position will be increasingly important when Spain enters the European Economic Community.

Nearly 30,000 ounces of gold were produced in 1981 at Jerritt Canyon.

Construction of the open pit mine and milling complex was completed late in the year, ahead of schedule and significantly under budget. Production will increase substantially in 1982, and FMC's 30 percent share in the project will contribute to earnings growth.

At full capacity, the mill is expected to produce 200,000 ounces of gold annually— enough to raise the total U.S. gold production by 20 percent. The Jerritt Canyon property has in excess of two million ounces of proven economic reserves, giving the mine a life of more than ten years. There are additional reserves that also may be economic to develop.

FMC was not previously in the gold business, but the company's industrial chemical products are largely derived from minerals. Exploration for new mineral deposits to ensure continuing control of raw material supplies is a critical part of FMC's industrial chemical strategy, and it resulted in the Jerritt Canyon gold find. FMC's mineral exploration program may lead to other gold discoveries, or to other new, mineral-based businesses.

FMC is the dominant producer of mobile airline cargo loading equipment.

Having gained an estimated 60 percent worldwide market share, FMC equipment is used by 163 airlines and 45 other customers in 61 countries around the world. Demand for loaders is expected to grow substantially over the next several years as deliveries of new models of wide-body aircraft accelerate.

FMC manufactures two types of loaders for wide-body aircraft, one to service the lower deck of passenger aircraft and another series to service the main deck of all-freight wide-bodies. About one-third of total air cargo is now carried in the lower decks of wide-bodied passenger aircraft, requiring equipment in addition to the needs of pure freight aircraft operators and freight handlers.

To prepare for expected market growth, FMC is building a new 240,000-square-foot plant in Orlando, Florida to manufacture loaders. Completion of the plant is scheduled for late 1982. The facility will lower manufacturing costs by significantly increasing the automation of loader production, and automation will also improve product quality.

To achieve and maintain FMC's target return on equity of 18 percent, selective changes must be made in the company's portfolio of businesses.

A major step in this ongoing process was accomplished in 1981 with the sale of the Power Transmission Group, comprising the Bearing, Chain, Drive, and Power Control Divisions. Sale of the Power Transmission Group generated nearly $105 million of cash, after taxes, to support growth in businesses with higher rates of return.

Other divestitures during 1981 were the Engineered Systems Division of the Material Handling Group, the European operations of the Sweeper Division and a small South African operation which manufactured material handling equipment. FMC's minority interest in an Australian manufacturer of material handling equipment was also sold.

FMC is building a loader manufacturing plant in Orlando, Florida, to meet increasing demand for air cargo loaders that can service the new generation of wide-body aircraft. (below)

The first gold bar was poured at Jerritt Canyon on July 4, 1981. The mine and mill will reach full capacity during the second half of 1982. (left)

Products and Markets

Industry segments	Operating units	Principal products and services	Markets
Industrial chemicals	**Industrial Chemical Group**		
	Alkali Chemicals Division	natural soda ash; chlor-alkalies; barium and strontium chemicals	glass-making; chemicals and plastics; household detergents; institutional and industrial cleaning compounds; pulp and paper; textiles; water treatment; leather and rubber goods
	Foret, S.A.	sodium tripolyphosphate; phosphoric acid; silicates; sodium perborate; hydrogen peroxide; organic peroxides	
	Phosphorus Chemicals Division	elemental phosphorus; sodium tripolyphosphate; phosphoric acid; technical and food grade phosphates; phosphorus pentasulfide	
	Specialty Chemicals Division	hydrogen peroxide; persulfates; plasticizers and flame retardants; phosphorus chlorides; swim pool chemicals	
Petroleum equipment and services	**Petroleum Equipment Group** Fluid Control Division Wellhead Equipment Division	wellhead equipment; fluid control equipment; loading arms	oil and gas producers; oilfield service contractors; pipelines and terminals
Defense equipment and systems	**Defense Equipment Group** Northern Ordnance Division Ordnance Division Steel Products Division	military tracked vehicles; naval gun mounts and guided missile launching systems	U.S. and foreign national governments
Performance chemicals	**Agricultural Chemical Group**	insecticides, nematicides and fungicides	food growers
	Special Products Group Food and Pharmaceutical Products Division Marine Colloids Division	pharmaceutical ingredients; food additives	pharmaceuticals; processed food industry
Specialized machinery	**Food Machinery Group** Agricultural Machinery Division Beverage Equipment Division Citrus Machinery Division Food Machinery International Division Food Processing Machinery Division Packaging Machinery Division	sprayers and specialty harvesting equipment; beverage processing and handling equipment; food processing and packing equipment and systems; packaging equipment	beverage processors and dairies; food processors and packers; packaging industry
	Construction Equipment Group Cable Crane and Excavator Division Construction Equipment International Division Hydraulic Crane Division	truck and crawler-mounted cable cranes; truck-mounted and self-propelled hydraulic cranes; pedestal cranes; tower-gantry cranes; hydraulic excavators; logging equipment	nonresidential and nonbuilding construction; mining; logging; offshore petroleum platforms; scrap; general industrial use
	Material Handling Group Airline Equipment Division Marine and Rail Equipment Division Material Handling Equipment Division Material Handling Systems Division Mining Equipment Division	airline loading equipment; railcars and barges; bulk material and unit handling equipment and systems; air and water treatment systems; mining equipment	coal, steel and transportation industries; mining; power plants; automated manufacturing plants; water treatment installations
	Special Products Group Automotive Service Equipment Division Sweeper Division Turbo Pump Operation	automotive engine diagnostic equipment; wheel balancers and aligners; street sweepers; fire trucks; marine boiler feed pumps	automotive test and repair facilities; state and local governments; shipbuilding and repair

Financial Review

Sales
(Dollars in millions)
■ sales in U.S.
■ sales outside U.S.

Primary earnings per share from continuing operations
(Dollars)

Return on equity from continuing operations
(Percent)

Disposition of net income
(Dollars in millions)
■ retained earnings
■ dividends

Total capitalization
(Dollars in millions)
■ net worth
■ long-term debt

Capital expenditures and depreciation
(Dollars in millions)
■ capital expenditures
■ depreciation

Financial Review

Additional information regarding FMC's operating performance and financial position is presented below.

SALES AND EARNINGS

Sales of continuing operations in 1981 were $3.37 billion, an increase of $160 million, or 5 percent, over 1980. Income from continuing operations of $176.5 million was $35.8 million, or 25 percent, higher than 1980. Primary earnings per share from continuing operations increased 26 percent to $5.28. A review of sales and operating profits by industry segment appears on pages 4 through 7.

Order backlog

	1981	1980	1979
		(Dollars in millions)	
Petroleum Equipment and Services	$ 210.3	$ 168.7	$ 100.8
Defense Equipment and Systems	2,020.4	1,228.6	743.8
Specialized Machinery	491.3	587.3	811.2
Total	$2,722.0	$1,984.6	$1,655.8

The petroleum equipment and services backlog increased 25 percent in 1981, reflecting strong market conditions in all major product areas. The 64 percent increase in the defense equipment and systems backlog resulted from Bradley Fighting Vehicle contracts for fiscal years 1981 and 1982, and substantial new orders for guided missile launching systems for the U.S. Navy. The 16 percent decline in the specialized machinery backlog was primarily caused by a continuing cyclical decline in railcar demand.

Backlogs are not recorded for industrial and performance chemicals due to the nature of these businesses.

Research and development expenditures

	1981	1980	1979
		(Dollars in millions)	
Industrial Chemicals	$ 26.9	$18.2	$14.1
Petroleum Equipment and Services	5.4	4.3	3.7
Defense Equipment and Systems	6.4	5.6	4.0
Performance Chemicals	33.1	28.0	23.5
Specialized Machinery	29.6	33.9	34.8
Corporate	4.4	4.0	3.3
Total	$105.8	$94.0	$83.4

The substantial increase in industrial chemical research and development expenditures was primarily caused by development of solution mining technology for trona ore, the raw material for natural soda ash. Expenditures in the performance chemicals segment are principally directed toward the discovery and development of new proprietary pesticides.

Not included in these amounts are $66.6 million, $58.9 million and $69.0 million in 1981 through 1979, respectively, for research and development projects paid for by government and commercial sponsors. Most research and development activity in the defense equipment and systems segment is performed under contracts with the military services of the United States.

Interest expense

Interest expense increased $12.4 million, or 22 percent, as a result of a higher average level of foreign short-term debt during the year, combined with higher short-term interest rates. Increased borrowings were principally in Brazil and Argentina, and interest expense does not reflect the foreign currency exchange gain arising from borrowing local currencies in these high inflation countries.

Taxes

FMC's effective tax rate for 1981 increased to 31.2 percent from 17.5 percent in 1980 due primarily to a higher level of pre-tax earnings.

LIQUIDITY AND CAPITAL RESOURCES

Over the past three years, FMC's liquidity requirements have been provided almost entirely from internal sources—primarily net income, depreciation and, in 1981, proceeds from sale of the Power Transmission Group. During this period, long-term debt decreased $51.3 million and, as a percent of debt plus equity, improved from 30 percent to 23 percent.

At year-end 1981, FMC had $150 million of unused open lines of domestic bank credit and $150 million of unused domestic bank revolving credit agreements. These credit sources remain available and are more than adequate to back up the outstanding commercial paper of FMC and FMC Finance Corporation. The company believes it has substantial additional long-term borrowing capacity that could be used without impairing the quality of its debt securities.

Known cash needs in 1982 are $52 million of scheduled debt retirements, $56 million of dividends, assuming continuation of the current common stock dividend rate, and approximately $300 million of planned capital expenditures. FMC expects these cash requirements to be met by internally-generated funds.

Working capital

	1981	1980	1979
		(Dollars in millions)	
Current assets:			
Cash and marketable securities	$ 219.3	$ 126.8	$ 109.8
Trade receivables	494.7	465.7	427.9
Inventories	484.1	469.9	458.1
Other	127.7	105.1	103.7
Total current assets	1,325.8	1,167.5	1,099.5
Less—current liabilities	877.2	768.9	696.9
Working capital	$ 448.6	$ 398.6	$ 402.6

Working capital at year-end totalled $449 million, an increase of 13 percent over 1980. The increase in year-end working capital resulted from receipt in October of the proceeds from the Power Transmission Group divestiture, which totalled approximately $105 million after tax. Excluding the divestiture proceeds, working capital declined $55 million, or 14 percent, reflecting companywide emphasis on tight control and management of assets.

Capital expenditures

	1981	1980	1979
		(Dollars in millions)	
Industrial Chemicals	$115.6	$102.4	$144.9
Petroleum Equipment and Services	46.3	31.9	14.6
Defense Equipment and Systems	36.1	35.2	24.6
Performance Chemicals	21.4	27.3	17.9
Specialized Machinery	35.7	52.7	53.3
Corporate	17.1	10.4	4.8
Total	$272.2	$259.9	$260.1

Capital expenditures in 1981 increased $12.3 million, or 5 percent, from the 1980 level. Industrial chemicals is FMC's most capital intensive industry segment, and it requires substantial annual investment for plant improvements and cost reduction. In 1981, industrial chemical capital expenditures increased 13 percent, which included construction of a new sulfuric acid plant in Spain and purchase of a longwall mining system for the Green River, Wyoming soda ash operation.

Petroleum equipment and services expenditures increased 45 percent, reflecting continuation of a major capital expansion program. A new plant was opened in Stephenville, Texas, and expansions of plants in Brea, California and Singapore were begun.

Defense equipment and systems expenditures increased 3 percent from the high level of 1980. During 1981, major new capacity to manufacture fighting vehicles was completed at San Jose, California, and conversion and expansion of an existing FMC plant at Aiken, South Carolina was begun to provide parts to the San Jose facility.

Capital expenditures for performance chemicals declined 22 percent, due to the completion of major capacity expansion projects in 1980 and 1979 which will meet expected near-term market demand. Specialized machinery expenditures declined

32 percent, as weak demand in several major product lines reduced investment requirements.

Corporate capital expenditures increased 64 percent, primarily for continued expansion of research and development laboratories, and for centralized computer facilities.

Depreciation

	1981	1980	1979
		(Dollars in millions)	
Industrial Chemicals	$ 64.4	$ 54.2	$ 46.8
Petroleum Equipment and Services	10.1	6.5	5.0
Defense Equipment and Systems	14.3	8.2	5.3
Performance Chemicals	18.7	17.1	16.3
Specialized Machinery	28.8	27.5	23.8
Corporate	3.8	1.6	2.2
Total	$140.1	$115.1	$99.4

Depreciation increased $25.0 million, or 22 percent, with major increases in three industry segments. Industrial chemicals' depreciation increased $10.2 million, primarily due to expansion of the Green River, Wyoming soda ash operation. Petroleum equipment and services' depreciation increased $3.6 million, reflecting a major multi-plant expansion program begun in 1979. Depreciation in the defense equipment and systems segment increased $6.1 million, due to the addition of new plant and equipment for production of Bradley Fighting Vehicles.

Dividends

FMC paid cash dividends totaling $55.8 million, $50.8 million and $49.2 million in 1981 through 1979, respectively. Payments to common stockholders during 1981 through 1979 were $51.9 million, $46.6 million and $45.0 million, respectively. The percentage of common dividends paid to income available for common dividends was 38 percent in 1981, compared to 34 percent in 1980, and 31 percent in 1979. Payments to preferred stockholders were $3.9 million, $4.2 million and $4.2 million for the three years.

QUARTERLY RESULTS

The financial information for the first three quarters of 1981 has been restated for the adoption of Statement of Financial Accounting Standards No. 52—Foreign Currency Translation (SFAS 52), recently issued by the Financial Accounting Standards Board and described in Note 2 to the consolidated financial statements. The restatement increased net income and primary earnings per share of the first, second and third quarters of 1981 by $3.7 million ($.11 per share), $2.8 million ($.09 per share) and $9.4 million ($.29 per share), respectively.

The third and fourth quarters of 1981 include after-tax losses of $29.8 million and $7.0 million, respectively, relating to the sale of the Power Transmission Group and provision for the eventual disposition of the Outdoor Power Equipment Division, discussed in Note 3 to the consolidated financial statements. The quarterly information for prior periods has been restated for these discontinuances.

Quarterly financial information (unaudited)

(Dollars in millions, except per share data)	*1981*				1980			
	1st Qtr.	2nd Qtr.	3rd Qtr.	4th Qtr.	1st Qtr.	2nd Qtr.	3rd Qtr.	4th Qtr.
Sales of continuing operations	*$813.8*	*$834.7*	*$842.7*	*$875.5*	$801.4	$809.0	$764.2	$832.6
Gross profit	*$191.9*	*$197.7*	*$196.1*	*$220.8*	$164.8	$174.9	$146.3	$173.0
Income (loss) after income taxes:								
Continuing operations	*$ 41.6*	*$ 41.0*	*$ 40.7*	*$ 53.2*	$ 40.4	$ 40.3	$ 21.6	$ 38.4
Discontinued operations	*$ 3.5*	*$ 3.8*	*$(37.3)*	*$ (7.0)*	$ .4	$ (1.0)	$ (.2)	$ 2.8
Net income	*$ 45.1*	*$ 44.8*	*$ 3.4*	*$ 46.2*	$ 40.8	$ 39.3	$ 21.4	$ 41.2
Income (loss) per common share—primary:								
Continuing operations	*$ 1.25*	*$ 1.23*	*$ 1.21*	*$ 1.59*	$ 1.21	$ 1.20	$ .64	$ 1.15
Discontinued operations	*$ .11*	*$ .12*	*$(1.15)*	*$ (.21)*	$ .01	$ (.02)	$ (.01)	$ .08
Net income	*$ 1.36*	*$ 1.35*	*$ .06*	*$ 1.38*	$ 1.22	$ 1.18	$ .63	$ 1.23
Income (loss) per common share—fully diluted:								
Continuing operations	*$ 1.15*	*$ 1.14*	*$ 1.13*	*$ 1.46*	$ 1.11	$ 1.10	$ .61	$ 1.06
Discontinued operations	*$ .10*	*$ .10*	*$(1.02)*	*$ (.19)*	$ .01	$ (.02)	$ (.01)	$ .07
Net income	*$ 1.25*	*$ 1.24*	*$ .11*	*$ 1.27*	$ 1.12	$ 1.08	$ .60	$ 1.13
Dividends per common share:	*$ .40*	*$ .40*	*$ .40*	*$ .40*	$ .35	$ .35	$ .35	$ .40
Common stock prices:								
High	*$ 35¼*	*$ 35¾*	*$ 33⅝*	*$ 27⅞*	$ 31⅛	$ 24⅞	$ 29	$ 31¼
Low	*$ 28½*	*$ 29¾*	*$ 25⅛*	*$ 24¼*	$ 21⅝	$ 21¾	$ 23⅝	$ 24

Fourth quarter results

Fourth quarter sales from continuing operations of $876 million increased 5 percent from the $833 million for the restated period last year. Income from continuing operations of $53.2 million, or $1.59 per share, increased 39 percent from the $38.4 million, or $1.15 per share, in the restated fourth quarter of 1980.

Fourth quarter net income of $46.2 million, or $1.38 per share, increased 12 percent from the $41.2 million, or $1.23 per share, reported in the year-ago quarter. Net income for the quarter was reduced by a $7.0 million adjustment to the estimated loss on disposal of operations discontinued in 1981. For the fourth quarter, net income and income from continuing operations were increased by $1.6 million, or $.05 per share, resulting from the adoption of SFAS 52.

Sales in three of FMC's five industry segments increased compared to the fourth quarter of 1980. Petroleum equipment and services, defense equipment and systems and performance chemicals increased strongly. Sales of industrial chemicals were essentially unchanged from the year-ago quarter, and sales of specialized machinery declined.

Strong sales growth of petroleum equipment and services was accompanied by higher earnings. Continued expansion of oil and gas drilling and production combined with added manufacturing capacity led to record results. Defense equipment and systems sales for the fourth quarter increased sharply, as the production of Bradley Fighting Vehicles (BFV) for the U.S. Army began to accelerate. Defense equipment earnings also improved substantially as higher profit margins in naval ordnance operations, and volume-related gains in vehicle operations offset start-up costs associated with BFV production.

Sales and earnings of performance chemicals increased strongly, with gains in both agricultural chemical and food additive operations. Agricultural chemical sales benefited from a good early order program for Furadan® insecticide-nematicide, and strong food additive sales reflected market penetration gains overseas.

Sales of industrial chemicals approximated last year's level, and earnings declined. Soft industrial chemical markets reflected the sharp decline in U.S. Gross National Product in the quarter.

Specialized machinery operations recorded lower sales and significantly lower earnings, primarily due to a steep decline in railcar production. The market for new railcars was virtually nonexistent during the fourth quarter, and FMC's railcar facility stopped production in October, when the backlog was exhausted. Sales of construction equipment and food machinery increased slightly in the quarter, and the earnings performance of each improved, moderating the overall earnings decline for the specialized machinery segment. Sales of food machinery in the European market were higher, and increased demand for preservation equipment in the United States produced a favorable sales mix change which increased food machinery profit margins. Construction equipment sales increased moderately, but the market for cranes and excavators remained depressed.

1980 RESULTS OF CONTINUING OPERATIONS

Sales in 1980 were $3.2 billion, an increase of $189 million, or 6 percent, over 1979. Income before incomes taxes of $170.5 million was $9.0 million less than 1979. Income from continuing operations decreased slightly, and primary earnings per share decreased from $4.22 in 1979 to $4.20 in 1980.

Industrial Chemicals

Sales increased 12 percent in 1980, and earnings increased 34 percent. Excellent results were achieved in soda ash operations which operated at full capacity. Chlorine and caustic soda volumes declined moderately from 1979, but profit margins improved as a result of higher selling prices and increased manufacturing efficiency. Sales of barium and strontium chemicals increased moderately, but earnings declined due to selling price weakness caused by low-priced imports.

Phosphorus operations recovered from the severe shortage of electrical power experienced in 1979 at our Pocatello, Idaho elemental phosphorus plant, although the shortage extended into early 1980. Sales increased moderately, but earnings were lowered due to a substantial increase in the Pocatello electrical power rates.

Specialty chemical sales were only slightly above the 1979 level, as growth in most product lines was partly offset by the cancellation of several minor products. Higher sales resulted from market share gains in established markets and continued growth in new markets. Hydrogen peroxide sales increased despite the dampening effect of the U.S. recession on many established markets. Improved hydrogen peroxide sales contributed to significantly increased earnings, overcoming the negative impact of fixed-cost additions resulting from the opening of a new 60-million-pound-per-year plant in December, 1979. Good growth was experienced in chlorinated dry bleach products, led by strong export sales and continued rapid growth in Sun® brand swim pool chemicals. Demand for plasticizers and fluid additive products declined moderately as the recession severely curtailed several important end-use markets.

Sales of FMC's Spanish subsidiary, Foret, S.A., increased substantially, and profit margins improved. Strong demand for phosphates and hydrogen peroxide was the primary source of growth. Selling price increases and improved manufacturing efficiency due to higher volume produced higher margins.

Petroleum Equipment and Services

Sales increased 37 percent in 1980, and earnings grew 52 percent, as margins expanded in response to higher volume. U.S. drilling activity continued to grow rapidly throughout the year, and FMC's wellhead equipment sales followed the strong upward trend. Sales of fluid control products also increased substantially, reflecting both the increase in drilling activity and a higher level of oil and gas production.

Defense Equipment and Systems

Sales increased 23 percent in 1980, and earnings were up 17 percent. Sales of tracked vehicles grew through increased procurement of M113 family vehicles by the U.S. Government and friendly foreign governments. Earnings were aided by receipt of $8.8 million of initial fees associated with M113 family vehicles and Armored Infantry Fighting Vehicles to be procured by the Belgian government.

Sales of naval ordnance equipment also increased substantially, and margins improved. Outfitting new vessels for the U.S. and friendly foreign navies and retrofitting of existing ships led to record production of guided missile launching systems and gun mounts.

Performance Chemicals

Slightly lower sales and a dramatic decline in earnings reflected poorer agricultural chemical results, partly offset by improved food and pharmaceutical products results.

Domestic sales of agricultural chemical declined moderately, while international sales improved. Earnings were well below the 1979 level. Sales declined for FMC's two most important agricultural chemical products—Furadan® insecticide-nematicide and Pounce® insecticide. Furadan demand was hurt by the high level of short-term interest rates and low grain prices in early 1980, which caused dealers to keep their inventories low and farmers to cut down on their purchases. Sales of Pounce were affected by a smaller cotton crop due to hot, dry weather and competitive pressures that forced down selling prices. The earnings decline was also caused by a substantially higher level of research and development expenditures and expenses associated with continuing international market development programs.

Sales of food and pharmaceutical products rose 15 percent in 1980, and profit margins improved. Strong sales of Avicel® microcrystalline cellulose, particularly in the European market, were the primary source of growth.

Specialized Machinery

Sales decreased 5 percent in 1980, and earnings declined 46 percent. Lower earnings from food machinery and construction equipment operations were partly offset by increased earnings of material handling operations.

Sales of food machinery operations increased 9 percent in 1980, but earnings were nearly unchanged from 1979. Margin pressure was caused by lower sales of agricultural machinery and reduced international food project work. Higher sales and earnings were recorded by citrus machinery and food processing machinery operations. Sales and earnings were also increased by the 1980 acquisition of Mojonnier Brothers Co.

Sales of construction equipment declined 1[illegible] percent, and construction equipment operations ended the year with a loss. The sales decline was especially severe in excavators and larger-size cranes. The sharp increase in interest rates in 1980, combined with credit controls and the onset of the U.S. recession reduced demand substantially.

Sales of material handling operations declined 6 percent in 1980, but earnings increased. Weak demand for railcars and the 1979 discontinuance of certain environmental equipment operations offset improved sales in other material handling lines. Mining equipment earnings recovered from the strike-depressed 1979 levels, and earnings of material handling systems operations also improved substantially. Reduced railcar operations had a negative impact on earnings, but elimination of operating losses from the discontinued environmental equipment lines helped the overall year-to-year earnings comparison.

Consolidated Statements of Income

(Dollars in thousands, except per share data)	Year ended December 31, 1981	1980*	1979*
Revenue			
Sales	$ 3,366,744	$ 3,207,192	$ 3,018,401
Equity in earnings of affiliates	1,985	7,348	7,786
Interest income	41,177	21,164	25,454
Other income	13,369	3,441	3,510
Total revenue	3,423,275	3,241,145	3,055,151
Costs and expenses			
Cost of sales	2,560,174	2,548,178	2,402,352
Selling, general and administrative expenses	431,239	370,851	335,175
Research and development	105,761	94,064	83,373
Interest expense (Note 15)	68,295	55,876	53,218
Minority interests	1,078	1,650	1,500
Total costs and expenses	3,166,547	3,070,619	2,875,621
Income before income taxes	256,728	170,526	179,530
Provision for income taxes (Note 11)	80,173	29,773	38,464
Income from continuing operations	176,555	140,753	141,066
Income (loss) from discontinued operations (Note 3)	(37,029)	1,955	10,500
Net income	$ 139,526	$ 142,708	$ 151,566
Earnings per common share			
Primary:			
Income from continuing operations	$ 5.28	$ 4.20	$ 4.22
Income (loss) from discontinued operations	$ (1.13)	$ .06	$ .33
Net income	$ 4.15	$ 4.26	$ 4.55
Assuming full dilution:			
Income from continuing operations	$ 4.88	$ 3.88	$ 3.90
Income (loss) from discontinued operations	$ (1.01)	$ .05	$ .28
Net income	$ 3.87	$ 3.93	$ 4.18

*Restated for discontinued operations.

See principal accounting policies and other notes to consolidated financial statements.

FMC Corporation and Consolidated Subsidiaries

Consolidated Balance Sheets

(Dollars in thousands, except per share data)	December 31, 1981	1980*
Assets		
Current assets		
Cash	$ 11,127	$ 10,278
Marketable securities	208,138	116,547
Trade receivables, net of allowance for doubtful accounts (1981, $19,101; 1980, $18,825) (Note 4)	494,708	465,646
Inventories (Note 5)	484,106	469,935
Other receivables	99,562	70,100
Prepayments and other future tax benefits	28,204	34,956
Total current assets	1,325,845	1,167,462
Investment in discontinued operations (Note 3)	—	135,379
Investments (Notes 6 and 7)	181,290	117,471
Property, plant and equipment, net (Note 8)	1,199,961	1,115,451
Patents and deferred charges	15,344	14,046
Intangibles of acquired companies	16,422	17,361
Total assets	$ 2,738,862	$ 2,567,170
Liabilities and stockholders' equity		
Current liabilities		
Short-term debt (Note 9):		
Banks	$ 46,675	$ 59,741
Commercial paper	11,708	5,298
Total short-term debt	58,383	65,039
Accounts payable, trade and other	461,890	392,159
Accrued payroll	69,953	64,138
Accrued and other liabilities	203,318	175,027
Current portion of long-term debt	52,302	36,952
Income taxes payable (Note 11)	31,378	35,580
Total current liabilities	877,224	768,895
Long-term debt, less current portion (Note 10)	395,649	417,723
Deferred taxes (Note 11)	160,387	127,854
Minority interests	7,716	6,797
Stockholders' equity (Note 12)		
Preferred stock, no par value, authorized 5,000,000 shares; $2.25 cumulative convertible; preference value $83,547	10,443	11,597
Common stock, $5 par value, authorized 60,000,000 shares	163,564	161,721
Capital in excess of par value of capital stock	46,460	41,692
Retained earnings	1,117,866	1,034,161
Foreign currency translation adjustment (Note 2)	(38,030)	—
Treasury stock, common, at cost	(2,417)	(3,270)
Total stockholders' equity	1,297,886	1,245,901
Total liabilities and stockholders' equity	$ 2,738,862	$ 2,567,170
Commitments and contingent liabilities (Notes 14, 16 and 17)		

*Restated for discontinued operations.

See principal accounting policies and other notes to consolidated financial statements.

FMC Corporation and Consolidated Subsidiaries

Consolidated Statements of Changes in Financial Position

(Dollars in thousands)	1981	1980*	1979*
Sources of working capital			
Income from continuing operations	$176,555	$ 140,753	$ 141,066
Items not affecting working capital:			
Provision for depreciation	140,081	115,146	99,383
Provision for deferred income tax regarding non-current assets	47,968	33,099	25,612
Equity in earnings of affiliates, net of dividends received	8,751	4,004	(6,848)
Working capital provided by continuing operations	373,355	293,002	259,213
Disposal of property, plant and equipment	28,036	34,545	3,633
Proceeds from long-term financing	46,980	24,681	36,522
Other, net	(8,525)	10,511	7,366
Discontinued operations:			
Proceeds from sale	110,000	—	—
Other (loss on disposal, income from operations, deferred taxes, etc.)	(11,650)	22,883	(1,761)
Total sources of working capital	538,196	385,622	304,973
Applications of working capital			
Capital expenditures	272,150	259,900	260,075
Dividends to stockholders	55,821	50,823	49,167
Reduction of long-term debt	69,094	46,597	42,472
Increase in other investments	72,570	25,552	8,445
Foreign currency translation	18,507	—	—
Non-current assets of companies acquired:			
Property, plant and equipment	—	5,427	—
Other, net	—	1,335	—
Total applications of working capital	488,142	389,634	360,159
Increase (decrease) in working capital	$ 50,054	$ (4,012)	$ (55,186)
Changes in working capital—increase (decrease)			
Cash and marketable securities	$ 92,440	$ 17,038	$ (108,307)
Trade receivables	29,062	37,793	33,446
Inventories	14,171	11,806	48,667
Other current assets	22,710	1,338	21,592
Short-term debt	6,656	(19,638)	2,294
Accounts payable and accruals	(103,837)	(45,613)	(47,633)
Current portion of long-term debt	(15,350)	(8,660)	(25,836)
Income taxes payable	4,202	1,924	20,591
Increase (decrease) in working capital	$ 50,054	$ (4,012)	$ (55,186)

*Restated for discontinued operations.

See principal accounting policies and other notes to consolidated financial statements.

FMC Corporation and Consolidated Subsidiaries

28

Consolidated Statements of Changes in Stockholders' Equity

(Dollars in thousands)	Preferred stock	Common stock	Capital in excess of par	Retained earnings	Foreign current- translation	Treasury stock
Balance December 31, 1978	$11,628	$161,551	$40,727	$ 839,877		$(4,633)
Net income				151,566		
Stock options exercised			9			59
Incentive plan shares issued			238			948
Conversion of securities	(2)	91	402			
Dividends on stock				(49,167)		
Balance December 31, 1979	11,626	161,642	41,376	942,276		(3,626)
Net income				142,708		
Stock options exercised		30	118			24
Incentive plan shares issued			108			332
Conversion of securities	(29)	49	90			
Dividends on stock				(50,823)		
Balance December 31, 1980	11,597	161,721	41,692	1,034,161		(3,270)
Adjustment for foreign currency translation (Note 2)					$(12,485)	
Balance January 1, 1981	11,597	161,721	41,692	1,034,161	(12,485)	(3,270)
Net income				139,526		
Stock options exercised		135	520			
Incentive plan shares issued			493			853
Conversion of securities	(1,154)	1,788	4,111			
Dividends on stock				(55,821)		
Purchase and retirement of stock		(80)	(356)			
Translation adjustment (Note 2)					(25,545)	
Balance December 31, 1981	$10,443	$163,564	$46,460	$1,117,866	$ (38,036)	$ (2,417)

See principal accounting policies and other notes to consolidated financial statements.

FMC Corporation and Consolidated Subsidiaries

29

Notes to Consolidated Financial Statements

Note 1: Principal accounting policies

Principles of consolidation. The financial statements reflect the consolidation of all subsidiaries except those excluded because of the different nature of their operations, of which only FMC Finance Corporation (see Note 7) is significant.

Marketable securities. Marketable securities are stated at cost, which approximates market.

Revenue recognition for long-term contracts. Sales are recorded under most production contracts as deliveries are made. Sales under cost reimbursement contracts for research, engineering, prototypes, repair and maintenance and certain production contracts are recorded as costs are incurred and include estimated fees in the proportion that costs incurred to date bear to total estimated costs. The fees under certain Government contracts may be increased or decreased in accordance with cost or performance incentive provisions. Such awards or penalties are recognized at the time the amounts can be reasonably determined.

Inventories. Inventories are stated at the lower of historical cost or realizable value. Historical cost is determined on the last-in, first-out (LIFO) basis for all domestic inventories other than those relating to long-term contracts. Inventoried costs relating to long-term contracts are stated at the actual production cost incurred to date, reduced by amounts identified with recognized revenue. The costs attributed to units delivered under such contracts (except cost reimbursement contracts noted above) are based on the estimated average cost of all units expected to be produced. The first-in, first-out (FIFO) method is used to determine the historical cost for all other inventories.

Inventory costs include manufacturing overhead, less, for most inventories, depreciation, factory administration, property taxes and certain other fixed expenses.

Investments in affiliates. The investments in FMC Finance Corporation, other unconsolidated subsidiaries and 50% or less owned entities, including the FMC gold venture, are stated at cost plus FMC's equity in undistributed earnings since acquisition.

Property, plant and equipment. Property, plant and equipment is capitalized at cost. Depreciation for financial reporting purposes is provided principally on the straight-line basis using lives which approximate those permitted by the 1962 Internal Revenue Service guideline regulations. Because of the diversity of facilities, it is not practical to list the various rates that are used.

Maintenance and repairs are charged to expense in the year incurred. Renewals are charged to the plant and equipment accounts that have been relieved of items renewed or replaced. Betterments are capitalized. Gains and losses on normal retirements of properties are credited or charged to accumulated depreciation and amortized to income over the remaining life of the asset. Gains and losses on abnormal retirements are reflected in income when realized.

Patents and deferred charges. Purchases of patents are capitalized and amortized over their remaining legal lives. Debt costs are amortized over the term of the debt.

Intangibles of acquired companies. These intangibles represent the difference between the consideration paid for companies acquired in purchase transactions and the estimated fair value of the net assets of such companies. Intangibles acquired since October 31, 1970 are being amortized on a straight-line basis over periods not exceeding 20 years; intangibles acquired before that date ($10.6 million at December 31, 1981) are not being amortized, as management believes that there has been no diminution of value.

Equity in earnings of affiliates. Equity in earnings of affiliates has been reduced by the net after-tax interest paid to FMC Finance Corporation (see Note 15).

Income taxes. Income tax provisions are based on income reported for financial statement purposes, adjusted for transactions that do not enter into the computation of income taxes payable. Deferred taxes result from timing differences in the recognition of revenue and expense for tax and financial statement purposes. Deferred taxes are not provided on Domestic International Sales Corporation (DISC) income, as management intends to follow policies which are allowed under current regulation that will assure permanent deferral of this income. Additionally, taxes are not provided on undistributed earnings of affiliates or subsidiaries, as it is intended that such earnings remain invested in those companies or, if distributed, the tax effect would not be material.

Investment tax credits are recognized as a reduction of the provision for income taxes in the year in which the assets are placed in service.

Proceeds from the sale of tax benefits under provisions of the Economic Recovery Tax Act of 1981 are recorded as other income and tax effected at ordinary rates. The resulting timing differences between book and tax treatment are reflected as deferred taxes.

Retirement plan costs. Current service costs are accrued and funded on a current basis. Prior service costs are amortized and funded principally over 30 years from the dates such costs were established.

Earnings per common share. Primary earnings per common share are computed by dividing the net earnings applicable to common stock by the weighted average number of shares of common stock and common stock equivalents (incentive plan shares and stock options) outstanding during the year—32,677,145 in 1981, 32,495,379 in 1980 and 32,415,582 in 1979. Fully diluted earnings per common share are computed using (A) the average number of shares of common stock and common stock equivalents outstanding during the year and (B) shares of common stock issuable upon conversion of convertible debentures and preferred stock. The average number of shares used in the fully diluted computation was 36,551,207 in 1981, 36,732,084 in 1980 and 36,673,382 in 1979. The fully diluted computation also adds back to net income the after-tax interest on convertible debentures and eliminates preferred stock dividends.

Note 2: Foreign currency translation

In December, 1981, the Financial Accounting Standards Board issued Statement of Financial Accounting Standards (SFAS)

No. 52—"Foreign Currency Translation" which supersedes SFAS No. 8—"Accounting for Translation of Foreign Currency Transactions and Foreign Currency Financial Statements." SFAS 8 required translation of certain balance sheet accounts, primarily inventories and property, plant and equipment, at rates of exchange in effect at the dates the assets were acquired. The adjustments resulting from translation were charged or credited to income.

Under the new SFAS 52, all balance sheet accounts of foreign currency financial statements, except those in highly inflationary economies, are generally translated at rates of exchange in effect at the end of the period. The resulting translation adjustment is reflected in the balance sheet as a separate component of stockholders' equity.

Implementation of SFAS 52 in 1981 increased net income and earnings per share by $17.5 million and $.54 respectively, and resulted in a foreign currency translation adjustment to the December 31, 1980 balance of stockholders' equity of $12.5 million. Had SFAS 52 been in effect for 1980 and 1979, net income would have increased by $.5 million in 1980 and decreased by $2.2 million in 1979, the effect on primary earnings per common share being $.01 and $(.07), respectively.

Net income for 1981 includes an aggregate foreign currency transaction gain of $9.1 million, resulting primarily from the Brazilian and Argentinian operations whose economies are considered highly inflationary under SFAS 52. Foreign currency exchange gains which, under SFAS 8, include foreign currency translations and conversions, are reflected in net income of 1980 and 1979 as $4.8 and $5.1 million, respectively.

Note 3: Divestitures and acquisition

During the third quarter of 1981, FMC sold its Power Transmission Group and provided for the eventual disposition of its Outdoor Power Equipment Division. The Power Transmission Group was sold to P.T. Components, Inc., formed by private investors. The sale was effective as of September 29, 1981, with FMC receiving approximately $125 million from the transaction —$110 million in cash and $15 million in notes. Sale of the Outdoor Power Equipment Division to its management is currently under negotiation.

FMC recorded an estimated loss of $36.8 million on disposal of operations discontinued during 1981, with charges of $29.8 million and $7.0 million to the third and fourth quarters, respectively. The loss includes the write-off of $21.3 million of goodwill for which there was no tax benefit.

The consolidated financial statements have been restated to include the net assets of these discontinued operations in "Investment in discontinued operations" and their net operating results, along with the 1981 loss on disposal, in "Income (loss) from discontinued operations."

Revenue and after-tax income (loss) were as follows (see Note 11):

Discontinued operations

(Dollars in thousands)	1981	1980	1979
Operating revenues	*$215,216*	$275,180	$289,148
Income (loss) from operations	*$ (229)*	$ 1,955	$ 10,500
Loss on disposal of net assets	*(36,800)*	—	—
Income (loss) from discontinued operations	*$ (37,029)*	$ 1,955	$ 10,500

In May 1980, FMC acquired Mojonnier Brothers Company, Chicago, Illinois for approximately $20 million in a transaction accounted for as a purchase. Accordingly, the related results of operations have been included in the consolidated financial statements from the date of acquisition.

Note 4: Trade receivables

Trade receivables at December 31, 1981 and 1980 under long-term contracts and programs do not include any material amounts of unbilled receivables, receivables collectible over a period in excess of one year, receivables billed under retainage provisions of contracts, or claims or similar items whose determination or ultimate realization is subject to uncertainty.

Note 5: Inventories

The current replacement cost of inventories exceeded their lower of (LIFO) cost or market carrying values by approximately $366 million at December 31, 1981 and $294 million at December 31, 1980.

Inventories at December 31, 1981 included approximately $410 million ($258 million in 1980) of inventoried costs, at cost or realizable value, relating to long-term contracts and programs. Costs normally associated with general and administrative functions are expensed as incurred. There were no material amounts in inventory at December 31, 1981 relating to (1) the excess of production cost of delivered units over the estimated average cost of all units expected to be produced, (2) initial tooling or (3) other nonrecurring costs.

Progress payments deducted from inventories amounted to $284 million at December 31, 1981 and $189 million at December 31, 1980.

Note 6: Investments

(Dollars in thousands)	1981	1980
Investments in, and advances to affiliates:		
FMC Finance Corporation (Note 7)	*$ 58,949*	$ 56,978
FMC gold venture	*27,183*	11,404
Other	*57,040*	28,817
Long-term notes receivable and other	*38,118*	20,272
Total investments	*$181,290*	$117,471

Dividends of $10.7 million ($11.4 million in 1980) were received in 1981 from unconsolidated subsidiaries and affiliates, and credited to the related investments which are carried on the equity basis. Restrictions on the payment of dividends by these affiliates are insignificant. Income taxes have not been provided for FMC's share of the undistributed earnings of affiliates not included in the consolidated federal income tax return ($14.4 million at December 31, 1981). The 1981 amount for long-term notes receivable and other includes $15 million of interest-bearing notes resulting from the sale of the Power Transmission Group.

Note 7: FMC Finance Corporation

Under the terms of an operating agreement between FMC and FMC Finance Corporation, a wholly-owned subsidiary, FMC is obligated to support the earnings of the subsidiary so that its earnings before income taxes and fixed charges (interest expense and rentals) are not less than 1½ times its fixed charges. Such support payments have no effect on consolidated assets or net income of FMC.

Condensed income statement:

	Year ended December 31,		
(Dollars in thousands)	*1981*	1980	1979
Income:			
Interest and finance charges	*$66,445*	$53,190	$33,513
Income maintenance from FMC	–	–	1,730
Total income	*66,445*	53,190	35,243
Expenses and income taxes:			
Interest and other fees paid to FMC	*1,794*	1,602	1,720
Interest—other	*38,793*	31,225	19,618
Other expenses	*3,816*	3,666	3,683
Provision for income taxes	*10,071*	7,555	4,638
Total expenses and income taxes	*54,474*	44,048	29,659
Net income	*$11,971*	$ 9,142	$ 5,584

Condensed balance sheet:

	December 31,	
(Dollars in thousands)	*1981*	1980
Assets:		
Finance receivables, net (1)	*$369,070*	$344,337
Other assets	*2,546*	2,573
Total assets	*$371,616*	$346,910
Liabilities and stockholder's equity:		
Payable to FMC	*$ 11,501*	$ 12,631
Short-term notes payable	*144,380*	123,319
Other liabilities	*16,786*	13,982
9½% Notes, due 1983	*50,000*	50,000
Note payable, due 1984, ½% over U.S. Treasury bill rate	*25,000*	25,000
Note payable to bank, due 1986, floating rate	*25,000*	25,000
9⅜% Note, due 1985	*25,000*	25,000
8.70% Subordinated notes, due 1993	*15,000*	15,000
Stockholder's equity	*58,949*	56,978
Total liabilities and stockholder's equity	*$371,616*	$346,910

(1) Including $279.5 million in 1981 and $258.4 million in 1980 from financing products sold by FMC, which represent receivables FMC is obligated to repurchase if payments become delinquent.

Note 8: Property, plant and equipment

(Dollars in thousands)	*1981*	1980
Land and improvements	*$ 144,927*	$ 135,576
Buildings	*298,318*	282,718
Machinery and equipment	*1,480,994*	1,358,059
Construction in progress	*96,526*	82,354
Total property, plant and equipment	*2,020,765*	1,858,707
Less accumulated depreciation	*820,804*	743,256
Property, plant and equipment, net	*$1,199,961*	$1,115,451

Note 9: Short-term debt and compensating balance agreements
At December 31, 1981, FMC had $300 million of unused domestic bank credit lines—$150 million in open lines of credit and $150 million in revolving credit agreements. These lines bear interest generally at the prime rate and the open lines of credit were available to either FMC or FMC Finance Corporation to provide support for domestic commercial paper borrowings.

FMC maintains compensating balances, where required, generally in amounts equal to 5% of the open lines of credit. Total compensating balances to be maintained by FMC amounted to approximately $4.5 million at December 31, 1981. However, after considering "float" in certain of FMC's operating bank accounts, none of the December 31, 1981 consolidated cash balance was needed as compensating balances under these arrangements.

FMC maintains informal credit arrangements in many foreign countries. Foreign lines of credit, which usually include overdraft facilities, typically do not require the maintenance of compensating balances, as credit extension is subject to the availability of funds. At December 31, 1981, $46.7 million was extended to FMC pursuant to all of the above credit arrangements.

Note 10: Long-term debt

(Dollars in thousands)	*1981*	1980
Sinking fund debentures:		
3.8%, due 1981	*$ –*	$10,869
3⅛% convertible subordinated, due 1981	*–*	627
4¼% convertible subordinated, due 1992	*71,245*	74,922
4⅞% convertible subordinated, due 1987	*2,135*	2,702
7½%, due 2001	*59,999*	62,999
9½%, due 2000, less unamortized discount (1981—$723,000; 1980—$763,000), effective rate 9.6%	*99,277*	99,237
Note payable to bank, floating rate (average of 23.5% paid during 1981 and 19.2% paid during 1980; 8% maximum over full term under certain conditions), due 1981-1982	*30,000*	45,000
Notes payable to banks, floating rates, due 1982-1983	*23,510*	10,000
Pollution control and industrial development obligations, 5.7% to 11.8%, due 1982 to 2021	*118,895*	116,795
Other	*42,890*	31,524
Total	*447,951*	454,675
Less current portion	*52,302*	36,952
Long-term portion	*$395,649*	$417,723

As of December 31, 1981, sinking fund requirements were satisfied for all debentures. Aggregate maturities and sinking fund requirements are (millions): 1983—$26.4, 1984—$23.1, 1985—$16.0, and 1986—$18.4.

Note 11: Income taxes
Domestic and foreign components of pre-tax income from continuing operations are shown below:

(Dollars in thousands)	*1981*	1980	1979
Domestic	*$228,153*	$148,042	$166,525
Foreign	*34,968*	32,846	22,242
Eliminations	*(6,393)*	(10,362)	(9,237)
Total	*$256,728*	$170,526	$179,530

The provision for income taxes consists of:

(Dollars in thousands)	*1981*	1980	1979
Current:			
Federal, before investment credits	*$32,149*	$14,136	$12,628
Foreign	*15,018*	5,654	1,833
State and local	*9,419*	5,148	7,625
Investment credits	*(19,660)*	(7,799)	(21,018)
Total current	*36,926*	17,139	1,068
Deferred	*43,247*	12,634	37,396
Continuing operations	*80,173*	29,773	38,464
Discontinued operations	*(11,310)*	(1,402)	8,167
Total income taxes	*$68,863*	$28,371	$46,631

Investment credits utilized in 1979 include $9.5 million carryback to prior years.

Deferred income taxes were provided as follows:

(Dollars in thousands)	*1981*	1980	1979
Tax depreciation greater than book	*$36,335*	$20,356	$16,031
Investment credits	*216*	(11,898)	–
Interest capitalized	*6,395*	4,475	–
Deferred income on trade installment sales	*7,774*	(487)	10,497
Excess pension contribution	*(2,516)*	(7,913)	9,659
Changes in discontinuance reserves	*(5,436)*	–	(3,998)
Other	*479*	8,101	5,207
Continuing operations	*43,247*	12,634	37,396
Discontinued operations	*(10,290)*	310	1,760
Total deferred income tax provision	*$32,957*	$12,944	$39,156

The effective income tax rate applicable to income from continuing operations is less than the "expected" U.S. federal income tax rate for the following reasons:

	Percent of pre-tax income		
	1981	1980	1979
"Expected" U.S. tax rate	*46%*	46%	46%
Effect of income not expected to be subject to U.S. tax:			
DISC income	*2*	1	3
Equity in net earnings of affiliates	*1*	2	1
Investment credits	*7*	12	12
Percentage depletion	*6*	9	6
State and local income taxes, less federal income tax benefit	*(2)*	(2)	(2)
Foreign earnings subject to lower tax rate	*1*	4	3
Other	*–*	2	2
Net reductions	*15*	28	25
Effective tax rate	*31%*	18%	21%

The undistributed earnings of DISC subsidiaries on which no federal income tax has been provided amounted to $137.5 million at December 31, 1981.

FMC's federal income tax returns for years through 1973 have been examined by the U.S. Treasury Department and have been settled. Management believes that adequate provision for income taxes has been made for all open years. Income taxes have not been provided for the equity in undistributed earnings of foreign consolidated subsidiaries ($110.8 at December 31, 1981). Dividends of $6.6, $10.5 and $5.4 million were received from such foreign operations in 1981, 1980 and 1979, respectively. Restrictions on the distribution of these earnings are not significant.

Note 12: Stockholders' equity
Under FMC's 1981 Incentive Share Plan, officers and key employees may be granted contingent rights ("Plan Shares") to receive payments of cash or FMC common stock, or both. Each Plan Share has a value equal to the value of a share of FMC common stock. The maximum number of Plan Shares that may be awarded under the Plan may not exceed 3 million. Payment of Plan Shares is contingent on continued employment with FMC for a specified period (except for death, disability or retirement) and, as to senior management employees, on meeting certain measures of performance. This Plan is a continuation of a similar plan, FMC's 1973 Incentive Share Plan, which expired on December 31, 1980. At December 31, 1981 total awards for 510,575 Plan Shares were outstanding. The estimated payout value of shares awarded under the Plans, as adjusted for changes in the market price of FMC's common stock and the estimated effect of payment contingencies, is being charged (credited) to income over earnout periods of four or five years. The impact on income was $(.3) in 1981, $3.9 million in 1980, and $2.8 million in 1979.

Stock option transactions for FMC's Selected Employees' Stock Option Plans are summarized below:

	Shares available for option	Shares optioned but not exercised	Option price per share
December 31, 1979 and 1978	742,775	34,500	$24.25
Cancelled—1980	1,500	(1,500)	24.25
Exercised—1980	–	(6,000)	24.25
December 31, 1980	744,275	27,000	24.25
Exercised—1981	–	(27,000)	24.25
December 31, 1981	*744,275*	–	–

No further grants may be made under these Plans except to employees of companies or ventures in which FMC has, directly or indirectly, less than a majority voting interest.

Each share of the $2.25 cumulative convertible preferred stock is entitled to one vote, is convertible into 1¼ shares of FMC common stock and is redeemable at the option of the company at $50 per share. The convertible debentures may be converted into common stock at the rate of one common share for each $41.50 principal amount of the 4¼% debentures and $31.10 principal amount of the 4⅞% debentures.

The following is a recap of FMC's capital stock activity over the past three years:

	Preferred stock	Common stock	Treasury stock
Balance December 31, 1978	1,860,545	32,310,270	242,103
Stock options exercised			(3,100)
Incentive plan shares issued			(49,528)
Conversion of debentures		17,565	
Conversion of preferred stock	(444)	552	
Balance December 31, 1979	1,860,101	32,328,387	189,475
Stock options exercised		6,000	(1,275)
Incentive plan shares issued			(17,338)
Conversion of debentures		4,002	
Conversion of preferred stock	(4,585)	5,728	
Balance December 31, 1980	1,855,516	32,344,117	170,865
Stock options exercised		27,000	(44,531)
Incentive plan shares issued		127,010	
Conversion of preferred stock	(184,584)	230,721	
Purchased and retired		(16,670)	
Balance December 31, 1981	1,670,932	32,712,178	126,334

At December 31, 1981, FMC common stock was reserved as follows:

4⅝% convertible debentures	1,716,747
4¾% convertible debentures	68,650
$2.25 cumulative convertible preferred stock	2,088,665
Employee stock options	744,275
Total shares reserved	4,618,337

Operations by industry segment

(Dollars in thousands)	Sales Year ended December 31			Income (loss) before income taxes Year ended December 31			Identifiable assets December 31		
	1981	1980	1979	1981	1980	1979	1981	1980	1979
Industrial Chemicals	$ 948,137	$ 854,795	$ 762,273	$140,747	$115,623	$ 86,615	$ 820,524	$ 772,791	$ 710,231
Petroleum Equipment and Services	340,005	236,440	172,702	69,034	40,963	26,944	283,682	199,221	143,837
Defense Equipment and Systems	582,005	570,434	462,916	53,491	71,730	61,077	280,572	201,722	139,574
Performance Chemicals	434,390	362,055	366,133	54,283	(2,399)	32,275	293,762	291,013	289,159
Specialized Machinery	1,086,486	1,199,152	1,267,035	(5,466)	20,585	38,236	624,858	682,202	705,563
Eliminations	(34,479)	(17,684)	(12,638)	(1,147)	168	375	(577)	(845)	(998)
Subtotal	3,366,744	3,207,192	3,018,401	310,852	246,670	245,522	2,302,821	2,146,104	1,987,366
Corporate and other				(54,124)	(76,144)	(65,992)	436,041	285,687	247,483
FMC continuing operations	3,366,744	3,207,192	3,018,401	256,728	170,526	179,530	2,738,862	2,431,791	2,234,849
Investment in discontinued operations								135,379	156,307
FMC consolidated	$3,366,744	$3,207,192	$3,018,401	$256,728	$170,526	$179,530	$2,738,862	$2,567,170	$2,391,156

Under the most restrictive provisions of bank loan and debenture agreements, approximately $172 million of consolidated retained earnings as of December 31, 1981, was restricted as to payment of dividends.

Note 13: Segment Information

Effective with this year's annual report, FMC restructured its operations into the following industry segments: industrial chemicals, petroleum equipment and services, defense equipment and systems, performance chemicals and specialized machinery. The operations in each of these segments are described on page 20 of this annual report. All segment information for 1980 and 1979 has been restated for this realignment.

Industry segment sales include both sales to unaffiliated customers and intersegment sales which are recorded at normal selling prices. Income (loss) before income taxes is defined as total revenue less operating expenses. In computing operating profit, none of the following items have been added or deducted: general corporate income and expenses, nonoperating interest income and expense, income taxes, equity in earnings of affiliates not directly associated with a segment, or minority interests.

Increased interest income, proceeds from the sale of tax benefits, and gains resulting from changes in foreign currency exchange rates caused a decrease in these net corporate and other items from $76.1 million in 1980 to $54.1 million in 1981. Identifiable assets by industry segment are those assets that are used in FMC's operations in each segment. Corporate assets are principally marketable securities and investments in affiliates.

Sales to various agencies of the U.S. Government aggregated $451.4, $433.0 and $337.4 million in 1981, 1980 and 1979, respectively. These sales were made primarily by the defense equipment and systems segment.

Operations by geographic area

(Dollars in thousands)	Sales Year ended December 31			Income (loss) before income taxes Year ended December 31			Identifiable assets December 31		
	1981	1980	1979	1981	1980	1979	1981	1980	1979
United States	$2,999,278	$2,751,287	$2,624,710	$266,916	$198,620	$221,100	$1,909,654	$1,719,390	$1,634,373
Latin America and Canada	164,285	132,982	139,600	4,916	6,309	1,663	101,586	152,121	124,336
Western Europe	165,906	352,461	286,220	33,174	37,192	24,678	248,461	256,811	217,733
Asia, Africa and others	37,897	31,354	18,896	6,654	4,817	1,833	28,893	25,565	18,391
Eliminations	(170,562)	(80,892)	(51,025)	(1,608)	(368)	(3,752)	(6,753)	(7,783)	(7,467)
Subtotal	3,366,744	3,207,192	3,018,401	310,852	246,670	245,522	2,302,821	2,146,104	1,987,366
Corporate and other				(54,124)	(76,144)	(65,992)	436,041	285,687	247,483
FMC continuing operations	$3,366,744	$3,207,192	$3,018,401	$256,728	$170,526	$179,530	2,738,862	2,431,791	2,234,849
Investment in discontinued operations								135,379	156,307
FMC consolidated							$2,738,862	$2,567,170	$2,391,156

Export sales to unaffiliated customers by destination of sale

(Dollars in thousands)	Year ended December 31		
	1981	1980	1979
Latin America and Canada	$164,398	$156,906	$119,186
Western Europe	143,991	151,373	95,520
Asia, Africa and others	336,854	222,460	225,125
Total continuing operations	$645,243	$530,739	$439,831

Note 14: Retirement plans

FMC has retirement plans for substantially all domestic employees and certain employees in foreign countries. Pension expense amounted to $46.8 million in 1981, $38.4 million in 1980 and $32.4 million in 1979. The increase in 1981 is due primarily to increased participation in the plans. A comparison of accumulated plan benefits and net assets for all the company's domestic defined benefit plans is presented below:

	January 1,	
(Dollars in thousands)	1981	1980
Actuarial value of accumulated plan benefits:		
Vested	$431,808	$398,231
Nonvested	32,936	29,504
Total	$464,824	$427,735
Net assets available for plan benefits	$529,447	$443,091

The discount rate used in determining the present value of accumulated plan benefits was 8% for all plans.

The company's foreign plans are not required to report to governmental agencies pursuant to ERISA and do not determine the actuarial value of benefits. FMC also contributes to several multi-employer plans, where the relative position of each participating employer is not determinable.

Note 15: Interest expense

Interest expense is reduced by interest paid to FMC Finance Corporation (offset against equity in earnings of affiliates, net of tax) of $19.8 million ($9.1 million in 1980 and $7.2 million in 1979) and capitalized interest of $15.0 million ($9.4 million in 1980).

Note 16: Lease commitments

FMC participates in leasing activities as both the lessee and the lessor. As a lessee, FMC leases office space, plants and facilities and various types of manufacturing, data processing and transportation equipment. Leases of a capital nature are not significant and, therefore, are accounted for as operating leases. Leasing from a lessor standpoint (principally food processing equipment) is not significant to the business nor the consolidated financial statements of FMC.

Total rent expense under all leases not capitalized amounted to $46.2, $32.5 and $29.0 million in 1981, 1980 and 1979, respectively. Minimum future rentals under noncancelable leases aggregated approximately $67 million, as of December 31, 1981, and are estimated to be payable $17 million in 1982, $13 million in 1983, $10 million in 1984, $7 million in 1985, $5 million in 1986 and $15 million thereafter. These future rental payments have not been reduced by minimum sublease rentals of approximately $3 million under noncancelable subleases. The real estate leases generally provide for payment of property taxes, insurance and repairs by FMC.

Note 17: Contingent liabilities

FMC has certain contingent liabilities resulting from litigation, claims and commitments incident to the ordinary course of business. Management believes that the probable resolution of such contingencies will not materially affect the financial position or results of operations of FMC.

Note 18: Supplementary information on the effects of changing prices (unaudited)

In accordance with Statement of Financial Accounting Standards No. 33, "Financial Reporting and Changing Prices," FMC has prepared a supplementary statement of income and a five-year comparison of selected financial data, both adjusted for the effects of changing prices. The supplementary income statement reflects the approximate effects of changing prices on inventory, property, plant and equipment, cost of goods sold and depreciation of property, plant and equipment in terms of constant dollars (general inflation) and current costs (changes in specific prices). Both methods involve the use of assumptions, approximations and estimates. Accordingly, the resulting information should be viewed in that context, and not as a precise measurement of the effects of inflation.

Explanation and methods of restatement

Cost of sales — FMC follows the LIFO method of pricing substantially all of its domestic inventories other than those relating to long-term contracts. This method results in a better matching of current costs and revenue during inflationary periods since it assumes that the latest items purchased or produced are the first items sold. Consequently, substantially all "inventory profits" have been eliminated from earnings. No adjustment has been made for efficiencies that would result from replacing existing assets with technically improved assets.

Provision for depreciation — Constant dollar depreciation has been determined by restating the historical cost amounts of property, plant and equipment using the average Consumer Price Index for All Urban Consumers ("CPIU") by year of acquisition, and then applying historical rates of depreciation. Depreciation for current cost purposes was derived by applying historical rates of depreciation to the current costs of the applicable assets. The higher level of depreciation calculated under the current cost method is not allowed as a deduction for U.S. tax purposes. It is FMC's contention that the present United States tax policies do not adequately provide for capital recovery during periods of inflation.

Other costs and expenses and income taxes — Other costs and expenses and income taxes have not been restated to either constant dollars or current costs. Such items are already in average 1981 dollars, for the most part, and further adjustment is not considered practical or useful.

Gain from decline in purchasing power of net monetary amounts owed — During periods of inflation, holders of monetary assets, such as cash and receivables, lose purchasing power since these assets will buy fewer goods or services. Conversely, holders of monetary liabilities benefit, since the obligations will be repaid in dollars of diminished purchasing power.

Inventories and property, plant and equipment — Under historical cost accounting, investments in property, plant and equipment are made over an extended period of time and added

together as though the dollars had equal purchasing power. Since the purchasing power of the dollar has declined materially, the values are understated compared to the expenditures which would be required today to purchase the same or equivalent assets. Constant dollar accounting restates the original investment into dollars of similar purchasing power, while current cost accounting attempts to revalue the assets in terms of current prices. The constant dollar amounts have been determined by restating the historical costs using the average CPIU by year of acquisition. For foreign operations, the historical cost of property, plant and equipment was determined by the application of historical dollar foreign exchange rates as required by SFAS No. 8. Effective with 1981 financial statement reporting, FMC adopted SFAS No. 52 (see Note 2) which resulted in a $19.5 million reduction in the reported value of foreign property.

The current costs were primarily derived by applying various indices to the historical costs and adjusting the resulting values, where considered necessary, to the estimated amount expected to be recovered through future use or sale of the assets. Specially constructed indices were used for land improvements, buildings and chemical and mining equipment, while producer price indices of the Bureau of Labor Statistics were used for most of the remaining assets. Foreign assets were adjusted for use of indices applicable to the various countries in which FMC operates.

Net assets at year-end — The net assets in constant dollars and current costs were determined by adding to historical stockholders' equity the change in inventories, net property, plant and equipment, and monetary items resulting from application of the constant dollar and current cost methods.

Five-year comparison — Data presented for other than the current year have been restated into average 1981 dollars. These restatements were accomplished by dividing the 1981 average consumer price index by the prior years' indices, and then multiplying the historical values by the results.

Statement of income adjusted for effects of changing prices

(Dollars in thousands)

	As reported in the primary financial statements	Year ended December 31, 1981 Adjusted for general inflation (constant dollars)	Adjusted for changes in specific prices (current costs)
Total revenue	$3,423,275	$3,423,275	$3,423,275
Cost of sales [1]	2,431,140	2,435,101	2,435,101
Provision for depreciation	140,081	195,886	214,555
Selling, general and administrative expenses [1]	423,069	423,069	423,069
Research and development [1]	102,884	102,884	102,884
Interest expense	68,395	68,395	68,395
Minority interests	1,078	1,078	1,078
Provision for income taxes	80,173	80,173	80,173
Total costs, expenses and income taxes	3,246,720	3,308,486	3,325,155
Income from continuing operations	$ 176,555	$ 114,789	$ 98,120
Gain from decline in purchasing power of net monetary amounts owed		$ 38,774	$ 38,774
Increase in general price level of inventories and property, plant and equipment held during the year			$ 232,866
Effect of increase in specific prices (current cost) [2]			$ 206,431
Excess of increase in general price level over the increase in specific prices			$ 26,435

(1) Excludes depreciation of $129.0 million from cost of sales, $8.2 million from selling and administrative, and $2.9 million from research and development.
(2) At December 31, 1981, current cost of inventory was $849.8 million and current cost of properties, net of depreciation, was $1,871 million.

Five-year comparison of selected supplementary financial data adjusted for effects of changing prices, in average 1981 dollars

(Dollars in thousands, except per-share data) Years ended December 31,

	1981	1980	1979	1978	1977
Total revenue	$3,423,275	$3,578,655	$3,629,476	$3,778,415	$3,203,247
Historical cost information adjusted for general inflation:					
Income from continuing operations	$ 114,789	$ 87,598	$ 122,505		
Income from continuing operations per common share	$ 3.39	$ 2.55	$ 3.62		
Net assets at year-end	$2,106,962	$2,079,523	$1,980,075		
Current cost information:					
Income from continuing operations	$ 98,120	$ 72,943	$ 106,073		
Income from continuing operations per common share	$ 2.88	$ 2.10	$ 3.11		
Excess of increase in general price level over the increase in specific prices	$ 26,435	$ 18,639	$ 57,632		
Net assets at year-end	$2,567,699	$2,256,817	$2,209,252		
Gain from decline in purchasing power of net amounts owed	$ 38,774	$ 46,135	$ 42,796		
Cash dividends declared per common share	$ 1.69	$ 1.60	$ 1.78	$ 1.74	$ 1.66
Market price per common share at year-end	$ 25.63	$ 33.67	$ 32.59	$ 33.82	$ 33.41
Average CPIU	272.5	246.8	217.4	195.4	181.5

Accountants' Report

The Board of Directors and Stockholders, FMC Corporation:

We have examined the consolidated balance sheets of FMC Corporation and consolidated subsidiaries as of December 31, 1981 and 1980 and the related statements of income, stockholders' equity and changes in financial position for each of the years in the three-year period ended December 31, 1981. Our examinations were made in accordance with generally accepted auditing standards and, accordingly, included such tests of the accounting records and such other auditing procedures as we considered necessary in the circumstances.

In our opinion, the aforementioned financial statements present fairly the financial position of FMC Corporation and consolidated subsidiaries at December 31, 1981 and 1980 and the results of their operations and the changes in their financial position for each of the years in the three year period ended December 31, 1981, in conformity with generally accepted accounting principles which, except for the change in 1981 in the method of accounting for foreign currency translation as explained in Note 2 to the consolidated financial statements, have been applied on a consistent basis.

Peat, Marwick, Mitchell & Co.

Chicago, Illinois
February 4, 1982

Management Report on Financial Statements

The consolidated financial statements and related information have been prepared by management, which is responsible for the integrity and objectivity of that information. The statements have been prepared in conformity with generally accepted accounting principles and, where appropriate, reflect estimates based on judgments of management. Financial information included elsewhere in this annual report is consistent with that contained in the financial statements.

The company's system of internal accounting controls provides reasonable assurances as to the reliability of financial records and the protection of assets. Internal control is maintained by the selection and training of qualified personnel, by establishing and communicating sound accounting and business policies, and by an internal auditing program which constantly evaluates the adequacy and effectiveness of such internal controls, policies and procedures.

The Audit Committee of the Board of Directors, composed of directors who are not officers or employees of the company, meets regularly with management, with the company's internal auditors, and with its independent certified public accountants to discuss their evaluation of internal accounting controls and the quality of financial reporting. The independent auditors and the internal auditors have free access to the Audit Committee to discuss the results of their audits.

The company's independent accountants, Peat, Marwick, Mitchell & Co., have been engaged to render an opinion on the consolidated financial statements. They review and make appropriate tests of the data included in the financial statements. As independent accountants, they also provide an objective, outside review of management's performance in reporting operating results and financial condition.

Arthur D. Lyons
Controller

Robert B. Coffman
Vice President—Finance

Ten-year Financial/Operating Summary

(Dollars in millions, except per share data)	1981	1980	1979	1978	1977	1976	1975	1974	1973	1972
Summary of earnings										
Sales	$3,366.7	3,207.2	3,018.4	2,673.2	2,096.6	1,883.1	1,743.9	1,418.6	1,188.6	1,011.0
Equity in earnings of affiliates	2.0	7.3	7.8	4.8	4.7	.1	4.4	13.2	8.8	5.7
Interest and other income	54.5	26.6	29.0	31.4	32.2	19.1	9.8	10.4	6.7	5.9
Total revenue	3,423.2	3,241.1	3,055.2	2,709.4	2,133.5	1,902.3	1,758.1	1,442.2	1,204.1	1,022.6
Cost of sales	2,560.2	2,548.2	2,402.3	2,104.4	1,607.2	1,425.9	1,340.8	1,090.3	898.3	757.9
Selling, general and administrative expenses	432.2	372.5	336.7	297.4	242.7	214.6	194.0	170.2	153.0	134.4
Research and development	105.8	94.0	83.4	63.9	52.6	51.6	43.0	43.8	35.1	29.4
Interest expense	68.3	55.9	53.2	45.3	37.1	37.0	37.4	32.9	18.8	14.7
Total costs and expenses	3,166.5	3,070.6	2,875.6	2,511.0	1,939.6	1,729.1	1,615.2	1,337.2	1,105.2	936.4
Income before income taxes and extraordinary items	256.7	170.5	179.6	198.4	193.9	173.2	142.9	105.0	98.9	86.2
Provision for income taxes	80.2	29.8	38.5	65.6	73.3	64.8	45.2	28.5	29.9	28.3
Income from continuing operations before extraordinary items	176.5	140.7	141.1	132.8	120.6	108.4	97.7	76.5	69.0	57.9
Income (loss) from discontinued operations, net of income taxes	(37.0)	2.0	10.5	8.1	—	(28.2)	10.5	4.4	10.2	11.2
Income before extraordinary items	139.5	142.7	151.6	140.9	120.6	80.2	108.2	80.9	79.2	69.1
Extraordinary items, net of income taxes	—	—	—	—	—	—	—	—	—	(20.0)
Net income	$ 139.5	142.7	151.6	140.9	120.6	80.2	108.2	80.9	79.2	49.1
Total dividends	$ 55.8	50.8	49.2	44.3	39.4	36.1	34.2	33.5	31.9	31.1
Share data										
Average number of shares used in earnings per share computations (thousands):										
Primary	32,677	32,495	32,416	32,399	32,250	32,163	32,091	31,958	32,048	31,971
Fully diluted	36,551	36,732	36,673	36,873	36,838	37,095	37,052	36,911	37,013	34,660
Primary earnings (loss) per share:										
Continuing operations	$ 5.28	4.20	4.22	3.97	3.60	3.24	2.91	2.26	2.02	1.68
Discontinued operations	(1.13)	.06	.33	.25	—	(.88)	.33	.14	.32	.35
Income before extraordinary items	$ 4.15	4.26	4.55	4.22	3.60	2.36	3.24	2.40	2.34	2.03
Net income	$ 4.15	4.26	4.55	4.22	3.60	2.36	3.24	2.40	2.34	1.40
Earnings per share assuming full dilution:										
Continuing operations	$ 4.88	3.88	3.90	3.65	3.33	2.98	2.70	2.14	1.93	1.62
Income before extraordinary items	$ 3.87	3.93	4.18	3.87	3.33	2.22	2.98	2.25	2.20	1.94
Net income	$ 3.87	3.93	4.18	3.87	3.33	2.22	2.98	2.25	2.20	1.36
Dividends per common share	1.60	1.45	1.40	1.25	1.10	1.00	.94	.92	.86⅜	.85
Book value per common share	$ 37.27	35.84	32.99	29.82	26.81	24.27	22.89	20.57	19.09	17.69
Financial position at year-end										
Working capital	$ 448.6	398.6	402.6	457.8	479.8	466.9	276.4	160.3	251.5	199.3
Property, plant and equipment, at cost	$2,020.7	1,858.7	1,677.9	1,449.4	1,284.1	1,096.2	1,014.0	883.1	756.7	678.9
Accumulated depreciation	$ 820.8	743.3	675.0	603.5	524.2	473.2	436.7	408.5	400.1	368.4
Total assets	$2,738.9	2,567.2	2,391.2	2,213.3	2,090.6	1,880.2	1,759.1	1,601.2	1,308.6	1,123.6
Long-term debt	$ 395.6	417.7	441.0	446.9	465.8	456.1	457.4	338.2	300.4	211.4
Stockholders' equity	$1,297.9	1,245.9	1,153.3	1,049.1	951.7	868.2	823.3	749.1	701.8	659.2
Other data										
Income from continuing operations before extraordinary items as a percent of sales	5.2%	4.4%	4.7%	5.0%	5.8%	5.8%	5.6%	5.4%	5.8%	5.7%
Net income as a percent of average stockholders' equity	11.0%	11.9%	13.8%	14.1%	13.3%	9.5%	13.8%	11.1%	11.6%	7.6%
Capital expenditures	$ 272.2	259.9	260.1	176.6	151.6	108.5	158.1	155.8	85.9	79.2
Provision for depreciation	$ 140.1	115.1	99.4	90.8	71.0	56.2	46.5	39.1	40.9	27.3
Employees at year-end	38,940	38,987	40,984	40,382	37,914	33,150	33,187	34,143	31,703	28,850
Stockholders of record at year-end, common and preferred	39,961	40,177	39,738	38,742	38,916	38,936	41,717	41,257	39,960	39,302

Income data for 1974 are after deducting $31.5 million, or $0.98 per share, reflecting the adoption of the LIFO method of accounting for essentially all domestic commercial inventories not already on LIFO.

FMC Corporation and Consolidated Subsidiaries

Officers

Robert H. Malott
*Chairman of the Board and
Chief Executive Officer*

Raymond C. Tower
President and Chief Operating Officer

Thomas T. Bamford
Vice President—Research and Development

Robert N. Burt
*Vice President
General Manager—Agricultural
Chemical Group*

W. Glenn Bush
*Vice President
General Manager—Material Handling Group*

Philip S. Devirian
Vice President

John R. Furrer
Vice President—Corporate Development

Patrick J. Head
Vice President and General Counsel

Robert B. Hoffman
Vice President—Finance

Charles H. Johnson
General Manager—Industrial Chemical Group

Charles T. Jones
*Vice President
General Manager—Defense Equipment Group*

Robert E. Purcell
*Vice President
General Manager—Petroleum Equipment Group*

William J. Kirby
Vice President

Arthur D. Lyons
Controller

James A. McClung
Vice President—International

John F. McKeon
*Vice President
General Manager—
Construction Equipment Group*

Robert McLellan
Vice President—Government Affairs

William A. McMinn
Vice President

Peter Perkins
General Manager—Food Machinery Group

Robert E. Purcell
*Vice President
General Manager—Special Products Group*

Sherman K. Reed
Vice President

Bart R. van Eck
Vice President, Treasurer and Secretary

Board of Directors

Robert H. Malott[1,3]
*Chairman of the Board
and Chief Executive Officer*

William W. Boeschenstein[5,0]
*Chairman and President,
Owens-Corning Fiberglas Corporation*

B. A. Bridgewater, Jr.[2,4]
*President,
Brown Group, Inc.*

John J. Cardwell[4,5]
*President and Chief Operating Officer
Consolidated Foods Corporation*

Paul L. Davies, Jr.[1,2,3]
*Partner,
law firm of Pillsbury, Madison & Sutro*

Robert W. Hubner[3,4]
*Consultant and former Senior Vice President,
International Business Machines Corporation*

Henry Kearns[5]
*Chairman and President,
Kearns International*

Edward J. Leckler[3,5]
*Former Chairman of the Board,
Abbott Laboratories*

John J. Nevin[1]
*Chairman and President,
Firestone Tire & Rubber Co.*

Charles B. Stauffacher[2]
Financial Consultant

Motley P. Thompson[2,3]
*President and Chief Executive Officer,
Baldwin-United Corporation*

Raymond C. Tower
President and Chief Operating Officer

[1] *Executive Committee*
[2] *Compensation and Organization Committee*
[3] *Audit Committee*
[4] *Public Policy Committee*
[5] *Nominating and Board Procedures Committee*

Executive Offices
FMC Corporation
200 East Randolph Drive
Chicago, Illinois 60601

Major Markets and Operations

Industrial Chemicals
Industrial Chemical Group
Alkali Chemicals Division
Foret, S.A.
Phosphorus Chemicals Division
Specialty Chemicals Division

Petroleum Equipment and Services
Petroleum Equipment Group
Fluid Control Division
Wellhead Equipment Division

Defense Equipment and Systems
Defense Equipment Group
Northern Ordnance Division
Ordnance Division
Steel Products Division

Performance Chemicals
Performance Chemicals Group
Agricultural Chemical Group

Special Products Group
Food and Pharmaceutical Products
Division
Marine Colloids Division

Specialized Machinery
Food Machinery Group
Agricultural Machinery Division
Beverage Equipment Division
Cities Machinery Division
Food Machinery International Division
Food Processing Machinery Division
Packaging Machinery Division

Construction Equipment Group
Cable Crane and Excavator Division
Construction Equipment
International Division
Hydraulic Crane Division

Material Handling Group
Airline Equipment Division
Marine and Rail Equipment Division
Material Handling Equipment Division
Material Handling Systems Division
Mining Equipment Division

Special Products Group
Automotive Service Equipment Division
Sweeper Division
Turbo Pump Operation

Manufacturing, Sales and Service Operations in Other Nations

Argentina
FMC Argentina, S.A.
Filsan Argentina, S.A.*

Australia
FMC (Australia) Ltd

Austria
FMC International A.G.

Belgium
FMC Europe, S.A.
FMC Food Machinery Europe, N.V.
FMC International A.G.

Brazil
FMC do Brasil, S.A.
Molyomite Industria de Maquinas, Ltda

Canada
FMC of Canada, Ltd
FMC Finance, Ltd*
Marine Colloids, Ltd*

Costa Rica
FMC International, A.G.

Dublin
FMC International, A.G.

France
FMC Europe, S.A.
FMC Food Machinery France, S.A.

Germany
FMC Machinery (Germany) GmbH.

Greece
FMC Hellas EPE*
FMC International, A.G.

Guatemala
FMC Guatemala, S.A.

Hong Kong
FMC Far East, Ltd*

Ireland
FMC (Ireland) Ltd.
FMC International, A.G.

Italy
FMC S.p.A.
FMC Food Machinery Italy, S.p.A.
FMC Packaging Machinery, S.p.A.

Ivory Coast
FMC International, A.G.

Japan
FMC Far East, Ltd*
Tokai Denka Kogyo, K.K.*

Korea
FMC International A.G.

Korea
FMC International A.G.

Mexico
Electro Quimica Mexicana, S.A.*
FMC de Mexico, S.A. de C.V.*
FMC Agroquimica de Mexico, S.A. de R.L.
de C.V.*

Netherlands
FMC Nederland, B.V.

Philippines
FMC International, A.G.
Marine Colloids (Philippines) Inc*

Saudi Arabia
FMC Saudi Arabia, Ltd*

Singapore
FMC Southeast Asia Pte. Ltd

South Africa
FMC South Africa (Pty) Ltd

Spain
FMC Spain, S.A.
Foret, S.A.
Tarros Intraluminales Industries Sales, S.A.

Switzerland
FMC International A.G.

Thailand
FMC Agricultural Chemicals Thai Ltd.

United Kingdom
FMC Corporation (UK), Ltd.
Oilfax-Chem, Ltd*

Venezuela
Tripoliven, C.A.*

*Unconsolidated